FROM
Lesson Plans
───── TO ─────
Power Struggles
Grades 6–12

*In memory of my brother
and first teacher, Everett Harris Trop*

FROM
Lesson Plans
— TO —
Power Struggles

Grades 6–12

Classroom Management
Strategies for
NEW TEACHERS

JUNE TROP ZUCKERMAN

CORWIN
A SAGE Company

For information:

Corwin
A SAGE Company
2455 Teller Road
Thousand Oaks, California 91320
(800) 233-9936
Fax: (800) 417-2466
www.corwinpress.com

SAGE India Pvt. Ltd.
B 1/I 1 Mohan Cooperative
  Industrial Area
Mathura Road, New Delhi 110 044
India

SAGE Ltd.
1 Oliver's Yard
55 City Road
London EC1Y 1SP
United Kingdom

SAGE Asia-Pacific Pte. Ltd.
33 Pekin Street #02-01
Far East Square
Singapore 048763

Printed in the United States of America

Library of Congress Cataloging-in-Publication Data

Zuckerman, June Trop.
From lesson plans to power struggles, grades 6–12 : classroom management strategies for new teachers / June Trop Zuckerman.
     p. cm.
Includes bibliographical references and index.
ISBN 978-1-4129-6877-5 (cloth)
ISBN 978-1-4129-6878-2 (pbk.)
    1. Classroom management. 2. Classroom management—Anecdotes. 3. Teachers—Anecdotes. I. Title.

LB3013.Z78 2009
371.102'4—dc22   2009014369

This book is printed on acid-free paper.

09   10   11   12   13   10 9 8 7 6 5 4 3 2 1

Acquisitions Editor:	Jessica Allan
Editorial Assistant:	Joanna Coelho
Production Editor:	Jane Haenel
Copy Editor:	Cheryl Rivard
Typesetter:	C&M Digitals (P) Ltd.
Proofreader:	Susan Schon
Cover and Graphic Designer:	Michael Dubowe

Contents

Foreword

This is a book of real stories, of real people, in real classrooms, stories that resonate deeply with anyone who has spent any time with novice teachers. There are characters, both students and teachers, whom we have met again and again, and situations we know like the back of our hands. Novice teachers will, in these pages, meet and recognize themselves, their teacher education classmates, and their adolescent students. This book has that level of immediacy.

The focus of the book is clear, and the organization makes the lessons to be learned lucid. There is, in the arrangement of chapters, a list of things novice teachers can do and think about when their best imaginings seem to fall apart in the reality of their classroom or when they are faced with a behavior they have never seen before. It will be a useful and quick reference book for novices. As teacher educators, we often say there is no point in teachers claiming the authority they have in the classroom unless they also have a set of activities for their students to build some understanding, in short, unless they have a well-designed lesson plan. We also know, with the author, that a well-planned lesson is necessary but not sufficient for an effective lesson, for the implementation of a plan requires teachers to manage space, time, materials, and people. The arrangement of chapters clarifies and supports this distinction for novice teachers.

In the extensive preface, Professor Zuckerman makes the argument for why she chose these stories and why she presents them in this format. The preface is a must-read as the grounding for both the stories and the structure of the book.

Readers will see that, for her, a well-managed classroom is best imagined not with a mind-set of discipline and punishment but rather from the stance of a teacher in a "learning habitat" (Zuckerman, personal communication). She has worked extensively with novice teachers and encountered with them a common wisdom in action. This wisdom is that when novice teachers practice effective classroom management, it no longer occupies an urgent place in conversation for them, but when there is little practice of management principles, nothing else of teaching seems more urgent to discuss. For novice teachers who find themselves in that phase, this quick source of guidance and suggestions will be a much-appreciated support, a place to go at the end of a tough day for some immediate ideas about how to approach seventh period tomorrow.

This book is not a list of strategies, a "What to Do When Times are Bad" list, although there is an extensive list of things teachers can try. Rather, it is a series of cases where novice teachers each describe and then reflect on their classroom situation. Through reflection, they figure out what big-picture problem they are wrestling with and how to respond to it. It is through this deep awareness of their own story that they develop. Teacher Jenny says, "Looking back, I see that I had been under the impression that it was my fault the students were acting out. . . . So I need to work on strategies to advance the lesson and avoid taking their misbehaviors personally." It is one thing for teacher educators and mentors to advise a novice teacher to resist taking students' misbehaviors personally; it is another for Jenny herself to realize that she was not only taking them personally but also taking the blame. Now she may be ready to address the situation, not the shortcomings of her students.

Crucial to these stories, of course, is the back story of the teacher preparation coursework in which the novice teachers learned about and discussed the theoretical groundings for solving such problems. In their stories, they are coming to understand these groundings well enough to call on them during their work with adolescents. Professor Zuckerman uses their stories to make the practical knowledge of teaching explicit in the realm of the theoretical and to enable other novice teachers to uncover what is really there.

The stories are pithy and poignant, as classroom stories always are. For example, Teacher Dina writes of the misbehavior in her classroom that "disorder spreads like a California wildfire." For another, what teacher has not had Leah's experience: "The persistent goal of my seventh-period beauties seemed to be to test my willingness to tolerate distractions." Teacher Ariana tells how a student noisily came into class late. Ariana asked her several times to sit down quietly, the student responding to the last request with a loud "f—off!" But the next day, the student came in to explain to Ariana and to apologize to her.

Then there is the story of defiant Debby, her teacher Mary, and one of their heated exchanges. Later, as she repented, Debby reported to another teacher that Mary was the first teacher to tell her that she had "potential." In these and other stories, the adolescents come into focus as more than a group of misbehavers—rather, as young folk in desperate need of being managed en route to learning how to manage themselves.

As we cross-reference the stories, we see similar solutions to different problems, and the same problem with different solutions. We see surface elements of behaviors and decisions and are helped to see the underlying principles. We meet Teacher Jason, who, when faced with disruptive behavior and inattention, asked, "Do you want to be responsible for this whole class taking a test tomorrow?" Then we meet Teacher Patrick, who found himself giving his students ultimatums in response to their inattention and misbehavior; namely, if they didn't behave, he was going to lengthen the homework or give them a quiz. Jason and Patrick were faced with the same problem of disruptive inattention and were caught in the same ineffective teacher response, invoking tests and extra work as punishment for the students' misbehavior. We learn, however, that these are cases of two novice teachers learning very different lessons from a similar experience.

The wisdom of the book is to help the reader see what motivated the novice teachers' responses and to see the lessons each learned. Jason understood anew that he needed to make effective plans, whereas Patrick understood that he needed to live the difference between being authoritative and authoritarian. And we see how the situations improved for both teachers and students as the teachers focused on changing the only behaviors that are, as the author says, under their control, which is to say, their own.

The stories in this book may serve all kinds of useful purposes for those involved in helping people to make themselves into teachers, by first of all helping them to put themselves in each story. Supervisors and mentor teachers may find the stories useful as a way to illuminate the principles behind the events. Those doing professional development, especially for teachers in their first years of teaching, may find the stories useful as cases for study and conversation. Teacher educators may find the book an invaluable resource for their student teachers, a well of inspiration, a way of affirming that they can, in fact, learn how to make a positive difference in the lives of young people in schools.

—*Jean Lythcott, PhD*
Theodore and Frances Geballes Clinical Associate and Lecturer
School of Education
Stanford Teacher Education Program
Stanford University

Preface

*F*rom *Lesson Plans to Power Struggles, Grades 6–12* is a book for novice secondary school teachers and those who foster their development. Its purpose is to help **novice teachers** improve their **classroom management** ability, that is, their ability to establish and maintain social order so that instruction and learning can occur. The term "novice teacher" refers here to a teacher with fewer than 3 years of teaching experience. Why a book for novice teachers? Because the novice years are crucial in establishing the pattern for a teacher's future professional development. Yet novice teachers all too often are left to sink or swim. Hard-pressed to survive, they fall back on the few strategies they know. This book provides an opportunity for novice teachers to learn the classroom management strategies that other novice teachers have used, ones that could also be useful for them.

Why a book about classroom management? Because 50% of novice teachers leave the profession, many citing classroom management problems as the major source of their dissatisfaction. Moreover, principals, instructional supervisors, and the public focus on classroom management when assessing the efficacy of a teacher. Thus classroom management is a pressing concern for novice teachers. This book is an account of the strategies that more than 100 student teachers used to solve their ordinary classroom management problems.

Each chapter is about a particular kind of classroom management problem and consists of one to several novice teachers' stories about managing that problem along with an analysis of the details, strategies, and practical principles that contributed to each teacher's success. Why stories? A **story** is a narrative that imbues a set of events with meaning. Accordingly, a story is both more appealing and more memorable than a list of strategies or principles for informing the immediate decisions in managing a classroom.

Second, whereas a list embodies **theoretical knowledge,** a story embodies **practical knowledge.** Novice teachers already have the theoretical knowledge to teach. That's the knowledge they constructed during their teacher preparation coursework, the knowledge expressed in generalizations. What they need is practical knowledge, that is, experiential knowledge, the knowledge that is bound up in the perception of details, the knowledge that is concrete and directly applicable to practice. By attending to others' stories about teaching, novice teachers transform their theoretical knowledge into practical knowledge. That's why stories are the next best thing to experience.

Why stories about novice teachers? Because the knowledge base of a novice is different from that of an expert. Not only do their respective repertoires of strategic knowledge differ, but the way they each perceive and define a problem differs as well. Accordingly, the strategies that a seasoned teacher would use and recommend are not necessarily helpful to a novice teacher, who cannot yet identify the dynamics within a classroom as the seasoned teacher does. In short, novice teachers need their own strategies to solve their own problems.

Second, novice teachers' stories help other novice teachers construct more realistic expectations about managing a classroom. Novice teachers enter the classroom with unrealistic optimism, believing their own personal attributes will shield them from the management problems that vex their peers. The harsh reality of the classroom, however, soon transforms their self-assurance into self-doubt, even shame. Consequently, rather than share their experiences, they retreat into professional isolation. Other novice teachers' stories confirm their experiences, restore their confidence, perhaps even their sense of humor, and help them to construct, along with practical knowledge, realistic expectations for managing their own classroom.

And why stories about student teachers? Because they are the rank novices. If a student teacher can identify a problem, formulate a strategy, and execute that strategy effectively enough at least to alleviate the problem even temporarily, then presumably another novice teacher with the same problem could recognize the correspondence and execute that same strategy. Thus the stories of other novice teachers, in particular those student teachers who solved a classroom management problem, are the best source of management strategies for another novice teacher.

The student teachers who contributed the stories for this book were preparing to teach in a New York State secondary school. They wrote their stories during their fifth week of teaching in either a rural, suburban, or urban public middle, junior high, or senior high school. Their stories are arranged in chapters according to the kind of problem they each addressed so readers can scan the Table of Contents for a chapter about their own problem.

The chapters are grouped according to whether the problem is a **lesson execution problem** or a **discipline problem.** Teachers' errors cause lesson execution problems. For example, an error in planning, preparing, or executing a lesson can cause directions to be confusing, activities to run short of the allotted time, or lessons to be boring. Each kind of lesson execution problem is assigned to one of the 13 chapters in Part I.

On the other hand, **misbehavior,** behavior the teacher regards as competing with, disrupting, or threatening to disrupt the lesson, can cause a discipline problem. Misbehaviors typically involve one or a few students rather than the entire class. Examples in this book include one or a few students violating a rule, talking a lot, or even cheating, fighting, having a tantrum, or **bullying** another student. Each kind of discipline problem is assigned to one of the 16 chapters in Part II.

Although no clear line divides a lesson execution problem from a discipline problem, and certainly one can exacerbate if not provoke the other, solving a lesson execution problem is simpler than solving a discipline problem. To solve a lesson execution problem, a teacher needs to change only his or her own behavior. On the other hand, treating misbehavior requires effecting a change in at least one student's behavior and often the teacher's as well. The purpose of this book is to help novice teachers effect such changes by providing them, through the stories of other novice teachers, an opportunity to reflect on and expand their own repertoire of classroom management strategies.

PERSPECTIVES ON NOVICE TEACHERS

Aside from my own perspective on novice teachers, I have relied on the work of Robert V. Bullough, Jr., author of *First-Year Teacher: A Case Study*. Through his compassionate portrayal of Kerrie, a promising first-year middle school teacher, the reader shares in the struggles, quandaries, misconceptions, fears, frustrations, disappointments, and failures as well as the insights, victories, satisfactions, and growth of a novice teacher. Examples of the practical principles I advance that derive from his work include the following:

- *Preparation and organization are crucial to the execution of an activity-based lesson.*
- *Novice teachers have difficulty claiming their power as the authority.*
- *If used consistently, a **routine** minimizes the time and energy needed to direct a regular classroom event.*

ETHICAL PERSPECTIVES

Teaching is a moral craft. A classroom management strategy must therefore not only promote social order, but the principles that justify its use must exemplify an ethical perspective. The ethical perspectives of the following teacher educators have contributed to my own perspective and guided the formulation of many of the practical principles in this book.

First, according to the late Haim G. Ginott (1972) in *Teacher and Child: A Book for Parents and Teachers*, the teacher is responsible for creating a positive emotional climate for learning and can create such a climate through authentic, solution-oriented (rather than blame-oriented) communication. Some of the practical principles that derive from his work include the following:

- *A teacher should be strict about students' behavior but permissive about their feelings.*
- *Instead of criticizing the actions of their students, teachers can safely express their anger by referring to their own feelings.*

Second, Alfie Kohn (2006a), in *Beyond Discipline: From Compliance to Community*, argues that it is better to foster a student's maturity (e.g., moral development, interest in learning, willingness to cooperate, or self-control) than force his or her compliance. Some of the practical principles that derive from his work are as follows:

- *A "working with" rather than a "doing to" approach promotes student maturity.*
- *Using threats (or bribes) to control student behavior undermines any potential for a mutually respectful relationship.*

And third, James Levin and James F. Nolan (2007), in *Principles of Classroom Management: A Professional Decision-Making Model*, advocate using the least intrusive management strategy so students can learn to control their own behavior. Some of the practical principles that derive from their work include these listed below:

- *Teachers need a systematic management plan ranging from subtle to progressively more direct and intrusive interventions.*
- *Rather than impose control, it is better to foster students' self-control.*
- *A private conversation preserves the student's or students' dignity, thereby forestalling a defensive or hostile response.*

Thus the strategies and practical principles in this book are grounded in the experiences, research, and perspectives of notable scholars in teacher education.

How to Read This Book

You can read this book in one of two ways: by either selecting a chapter for a particular problem or reading the book sequentially. Every chapter can stand alone. Each technical term (or grammatical variant of that term) is printed in a bold font the first time it is used in each chapter and then defined in the glossary. Moreover, the glossary includes an index so readers can locate that term in other chapters (see Glossary and Index of Technical Terms).

Likewise, every practical principle is italicized in each chapter and listed in both the Alphabetical Index of Practical Principles and the Topical Index of Practical Principles. Thus, by selecting a particular chapter, readers can get immediate help for a classroom management problem and, with a little more exploration, elaborate their understanding of a technical term or practical principle.

Each chapter also includes at least one supplementary note about and set of references for a concept related to one or more of the stories. Some references cite the literature in which the concept was first formulated. Others cite contemporary applications of the concept. Thus each chapter also has pointers for further study (see Index of Supplementary Concepts).

Alternatively, reading the book sequentially provides an opportunity to appreciate the range of novice teachers' ordinary problems and strategic options. First, readers can proactively formulate their own management plan, something novice teachers desperately need but, given their unrealistic optimism, neglect to do. Such a management plan would enable them to respond temperately and consistently whenever a rule or routine is challenged.

Second, readers can see how lesson execution problems or strategies interact with discipline problems or strategies. For example, Charlotte's inability to give clear directions (see Charlotte's Story, Chapter 4) prompted some of her students to cheat. Likewise, a teacher can obviate some of a **class clown**'s disruptions (see Chapter 15) by replacing whole-class with small-group learning activities.

Third, readers can recognize the roots common to various problems and accordingly manage them with a common set of strategies. For example, reading about how to manage a class clown (see Chapter 15) can help a novice teacher like Abby (see Abby's Story, Chapter 27) manage a student who persistently seeks her attention.

Whether selecting particular chapters or reading the book sequentially, for each story readers should ask themselves the following questions: How would I respond to this situation? Given the details of the situation, how would I justify my response?

How could I use this strategy in other situations? When would the strategy be inappropriate? How do my values and beliefs compare with those implicit in the use of the strategy?

So let's begin with a story about a student teacher who was anxious about managing her classes:

Cora's Story

I just started student teaching in a large urban district with a reputation for tough, hard-to-control kids. My friends and colleagues warned me that this would not be the district I'd want to stay in. All their comments made me anxious about managing the large classes of mostly minority students.

During these first few weeks, however, I have been teaching lessons with hands-on activities that have involved almost all the students. The head of the department recently observed me teaching a lesson on the color wheel, which I thought went well. All the students participated in the activities and seemed to understand the main points of the lesson.

When I met with the head of the department after the class, he said, "You seem to have the class under control, and I like the fact that you've created your own way to teach this concept." I was overjoyed because I felt he was endorsing the approach I believe in.

I am fortunate to be in a school where the head of the department has confidence in me and encourages me to teach in a way that makes sense to me. Because of the school's reputation, I was needlessly afraid of the classroom management challenges, but my lessons keep the kids engaged and reward them for their engagement.

Cora found that both the head of the department and her students were receptive to lessons with active learning opportunities. *An appealing lesson is necessary but not sufficient to preclude most discipline problems.* Because novice teachers have a limited repertoire of appealing lessons and little experience executing such lessons, classroom management is a pressing concern. The advantage of a well-planned lesson and the frustration that can come from an oversight in its execution are, accordingly, the subjects of Chapter 1.

Acknowledgments

I am grateful to my husband, Paul R. Zuckerman, for supporting this project as he supports all my dreams and for simply and unfailingly believing in me.

I am also grateful to my former students who, as student teachers, trusted me with the stories of their failures and frustrations as well as their successes and satisfactions and who granted me permission to retell their stories so other novice teachers might benefit.

Last, I am grateful to my editors and reviewers at Corwin for their enthusiasm for and criticism of this work.

PUBLISHER'S ACKNOWLEDGMENTS

Corwin gratefully acknowledges the following peer reviewers for their editorial insight and guidance:

Michelle Barnea
Executive Director
Early Learning Innovations LLC
Millburn, NJ

Dianne Evans Kelley
Assistant Professor
Cardinal Stritch University
Milwaukee, WI

Sammie Novack
Principal
Munsey Elementary School
Bakersfield, CA

Dr. Elisabeth Hess Rice
Assistant Professor
Department of Teacher Preparation and Special Education
The George Washington University
Washington, DC

Pamela D. Tabor, PhD
Math Coach/Elementary Math Specialist
Harford County Public Schools
Havre de Grace, MD

Dr. Bob Wyatt
Professor Emeritus
East Central University
Ada, OK

About the Author

 **June Trop Zuckerman** has had over 40 years of experience as an award-winning teacher and educator, approximately half of those years as a middle and high school science teacher and half as a professor of secondary education. Over the years, she has conducted countless classes and seminars for and about novice teachers and coached scores of them in their own classroom to improve their management skills.

With an EdD in science education from Teachers College, Zuckerman's recent research has focused on the mentoring of novice teachers, their classroom management strategies, and the practical knowledge they construct and communicate through storytelling. Her papers on these topics have appeared regularly in the *Journal of Science Teacher Education*, *Science Educator*, and *American Secondary Education*.

Now Associate Professor Emerita at the State University of New York at New Paltz, she continues to live in New Paltz with her husband, Paul, and use her extensive theoretical and practical knowledge of pedagogy to speak to and coach teachers at colleges and secondary schools in the region.

PART I

Lesson Execution Problems

The Advantage of a Well-Planned, Activity-Based Lesson

The first three **stories** in this chapter are about how a well-planned, activity-based lesson engages students, thereby precluding the management problems that frustration and boredom can generate. In the fourth story, the teacher explains how he planned not only the activities but the very transition between them. A fifth story demonstrates how confusing directions and the careless distribution of materials can derail even a promising lesson.

Ryan's Story

In preparation for my biology class on competition within an animal population, I placed paper strips of various colors on the walls of the hall outside the classroom. Some were quite visible, such as a blue strip against a white wall, whereas others were more difficult to find, such as a red strip on a fire extinguisher. All of these strips represented food that the students, as members of an animal population, would need in order to survive.

Prior to the search, I gave the students a 10-minute lecture on hunting techniques used in the wild. Then I told them to bring back as many strips as they could find in the 8 minutes I would give them. Without necessarily realizing it, they used some of the techniques mentioned in the lecture. And as the students experienced the struggles animals face in their search for food, they realized that the competition for resources was intense.

Now and then I still see a strip of paper in the hall, one that we missed during the cleanup. It reminds me that a well-planned and well-executed lesson, aside from enhancing the students' understanding, is fun besides.

Ryan's lesson generated enthusiasm because the activity was novel for his students. In addition, he made the connection explicit between the activity and the concept of competition so the activity could make sense to them. Undoubtedly, his students also appreciated his effort to prepare such a novel activity. *Students appreciate a novel activity as long as its meaning has been made explicit.* How could you add novelty to one of your own activities?

Jill's Story

For their study of animal nutrition, the students in my 10th-grade biology class were observing live hydra with their microscopes. Each pair had a hydra. While observing it, they each had to draw what they saw and label specific parts. Once they had done that, I gave each pair a daphnia for the hydra to ingest.

One pair of students was truly amazed and enthusiastic. Their hydra was ingesting its daphnia. They seemed almost proud of their hydra, especially when other students wanted to see it. They were far from the top students in the class. Actually, they were average to below average.

When it was time for the class to end, both students were so caught up in the lesson that they asked to stay. They had such an honest interest, I was really surprised.

(Continued)

(Continued)

I remember this event because it reaffirmed my belief that novel, hands-on experiences can reach students who might otherwise not respond to a lesson. It was also special for me because the informal atmosphere of the activity gave me a chance to interact with the students on a more personal level.

The excitement her lesson generated, especially among her low achievers, surprised Jill. However, in addition to having prepared a novel activity, she had assigned the class to work in pairs. *Having students work in pairs (with teacher support) is particularly useful for low achievers, who can then teach each other without the fear of making a mistake publicly.*

Henry's Story

I prepared a lesson for my ninth graders on how to identify the relative age of rock layers. I started the lesson with a **do-now,** where the students were to define some terms in their text that they would need for the lesson. I gave them 3 minutes, and while they were defining the terms, I projected a few diagrams on the screen.

When they finished the do-now, I asked several students to identify the structures in the diagrams that would be crucial to their understanding the rest of the lesson. Then I took about 10 minutes to review the homework because the day's activity would be based on that information as well.

Next I distributed a worksheet with a geologic cross section that was much more complex than the homework they had just completed. The students were to work in groups of three to answer the seven questions on the worksheet while I circulated among them to make sure they were on task and on track. I used about 13 of the 15 minutes I'd allotted for this worksheet activity.

Then, for us to see how well they understood the activity, I placed a transparency of the worksheet on the overhead projector and asked several "what if" and "why" questions related to the cross section. These questions took about 7 minutes. Finally, I closed the lesson with a summary, some comments about the next day's topic, and the homework assignment.

> My management strategy was to keep the students busy. I allowed a few minutes for the transition from one instructional segment to the next but otherwise maximized the instructional time available in a 40-minute period.

Henry crafted his lesson with a clear objective and the 40-minute time frame in mind. Through a series of instructional segments, he got his students settled, reviewed the homework, and focused them on the day's objective. Then he had them build and share their understandings in small groups, assess their understandings in response to thought-provoking questions, and finally attend to the lesson's closure. The advantages of such a segmented lesson are that teachers can (a) identify errors in their timing estimates and make adjustments during subsequent segments, (b) renew student interest and integrate latecomers with each new segment, and (c) gauge the usefulness of an activity for student learning and then, if necessary, modify the rest of the lesson.

Perhaps Henry's most important segment was his do-now. The do-now is a daily **routine** consisting of an activity each student is expected to work on independently for the first few minutes upon entering the classroom. The purpose of the do-now is to get, without supervision and even before the bell rings, every student ready to work. Accordingly, *the do-now must be an activity that requires students to sit down and take out their notebook, perhaps their textbook, and a pencil or pen.* The teacher takes attendance and otherwise prepares to launch the lesson during the do-now.

In addition to the do-now, Henry regularly uses other instructional segments, such as group work followed by an assessment activity, to structure his lessons. The regularity of this framework reduces Henry's need to repeat everyday directions and keeps the students aware of his expectations as each lesson unfolds.

How do you structure your lessons? A regularity in structure in no way diminishes your opportunity to keep the content of each lesson fresh. The only caveat? *Make the connection between instructional segments explicit to your students.*

Ira's Story

During one of my first double-period classes in the high school, I prepared about 80 minutes of lecture, interspersed with questions and small-group writing projects. I spent hours preparing my talk on fiction in film and included pictures, anecdotes, and artifacts from my memorabilia collection. I was able to keep most of the students engrossed by mixing entertainment with some important facts.

The two 80-minute lectures, almost back-to-back, left me emotionally and physically drained, however, so much so that when I got home, I needed a 3-hour nap. As much as the students enjoyed the lecture, I knew it would be impossible for me to perform like that regularly. So I vowed to plan more activities for the students to do, especially during our double-period classes.

I planned a test for the first part of the next double period and an informal group activity for the second part. I posted the directions for the activity on the board and, before the test, explained them briefly. I anticipated a problem, however. How could I, during our customary break after 40 minutes, prevent the sharing of test answers with those who had yet to finish the test? So I stated that students could not take their break until they had finished and handed in their test.

The transition between the test and the activity went smoothly, and, relieved to be doing something relaxing after the test, most students doing the activity were considerate of those still working on the test.

Ira not only balanced the activities for his double period by providing a relaxing one to follow an intense one, but, just as important, he planned for the transition between them as well. How could you balance your activities and plan for the transition between them?

Jason's Story

We got through the do-now quickly and began going over the directions for groups to dramatize some scenes from *Hamlet*. The noise became thunderous. So I asked, "Eric, would you like to take the rest of this period to talk to Kelly? Why don't we forget about this activity, and all of you can talk to your friends for the rest of the period while I make a test for this class to take tomorrow? Does that sound good?" Their response to this proposal was a chorus of disapproval. I continued with the directions, but occasionally I still had to remind them that I could schedule a test for tomorrow.

During the activity, I needed to call their attention to some specific details, and it was difficult to get everyone quiet. I called a student by name and asked him to be quiet. As soon as I looked elsewhere, he began talking again. I responded, "Joe, do you want to be responsible for the whole class taking a test tomorrow? Okay then, be quiet for a minute while I explain this." As soon as I turned my back, he was talking again. As I leaned over the desk, I yelled, "Joe, don't you understand English? I don't like getting in a student's face, but you won't shut up!" He stopped talking for almost a minute.

After reflecting on this lesson, I came to some conclusions. First, I should have been better prepared and more organized for the lesson. Then I wouldn't have had to interrupt the activity to get their attention. They needed many materials for the activity, and I should have had everything ready for each group. Also, the directions were complicated, and I did not have them printed on their handouts or telegraphed on the screen.

Second, I don't think it was a good idea for me to use the threat of a test as a punishment, just as homework should not be used as a punishment. And I know it was wrong to use sarcasm. Instead, I could have moved some of the students in Joe's group, the group that seemed to ignite the rest of the class.

I thought I was prepared for this lesson, but I learned that it takes a lot of preparation and organization to be ready for an activity-based lesson.

Jason planned a promising, activity-based lesson, but unlike Ira, he failed to prepare adequately for its execution. Noise became a problem for Jason as soon as he began to explain the directions, a clue that his students were getting confused from the very beginning. At that point, he needed to *address the situation, not the shortcomings of the student(s)*. For example, he could have said to the class, "This noise is unacceptable. How can we keep it down?"

Jason's story demonstrates that *preparation and organization are crucial to the execution of an activity-based lesson.* **Novice teachers**, however, do not yet have the repertoire of activities, let alone the foresight, to anticipate their logistical hurdles. Consequently, they face a plethora of **classroom management** problems. The following chapters present accounts of how a novice teacher dealt successfully with a classroom management problem.

Note: Contemporary Conception of a Good Lesson

According to the transmission view of pedagogy, students learn by acquiring information as the teacher or text transmits it. Contemporary theorists, however, view learning as socially constructed. That is, students construct their own understandings as they relate new information to their prior knowledge and then modify or validate their understandings as they exchange ideas with others. Accordingly, to a social constructivist, a good lesson would feature pairs or small groups of students engaged in reflective discussion to reach common understandings.

- Good, T. L., & Brophy, J. E. (2008). *Looking in classrooms* (10th ed.). Boston: Pearson.
- Vygotsky, L. (1962). *Thought and language.* Cambridge, MA: MIT Press.

2

When Your Lesson Plan Is Inadequate

The first two **stories** are about inadequate planning for the content of a lesson. The second two are about inadequate planning for the execution of a lesson. **Planning for the content** refers to the teacher's defining the lesson objective and then devising a set of activities in which the students can construct the knowledge in that objective and then, along with the teacher, assess whether they've constructed it as intended. **Planning for the execution** refers to the teacher's determining how (and sometimes when) to take attendance, divide the students into groups, distribute and collect materials, give directions, and so forth. Both kinds of planning are essential for maintaining order.

Inadequate Planning
for the Content of a Lesson

Brett's Story

Last week in my consumer math class, I was challenged to maintain classroom discipline. This class has 13 ninth and tenth graders, nearly all doing poorly and showing little respect for anyone in the room. The particular student who challenged me, Joe, had recently returned from a 5-day suspension. He has a well-developed physique and enjoys showing it off.

I began the class by asking the students to study for the quiz I was going to give them later in the period. At first, Joe didn't want to study, so I threatened to give the quiz to the class right then and there. The other students, however, convinced him to take out his notebook and study. After about a minute, he began to talk to the student next to him, so I moved Joe's seat to the back of the room. After about another minute, he began talking to the same student again, now from across the room. At this point, I told him to stop talking and study for the quiz. To this he answered, "What are you gonna do if I don't?"

I threatened him again, this time to write a referral on him. So he quickly quieted down because he had been told that if he got any more referrals, he could be thrown out of school.

I felt I took the proper steps. I knew from his other teachers that Joe's father has him on a short leash. So after moving his seat, I knew that the next step, threatening him with a referral, would work.

Instead of blaming Joe for disrupting the class's study time, Brett should have devised a definite review activity. *Activities in which students can work together, choose their task, be creative, use novel materials, imagine a novel situation, or relate a concept to everyday life appeal to students.* For example, Brett could have given his students a list of concepts for the quiz and had them form groups, each group choosing its own concept. Then he could have had each group create a poster, skit, story, or song to explain the concept and make a 1-minute presentation of that concept to the rest of the class. (See the comments following Chad's Story, Chapter 5, for how a teacher could execute such an activity, and for an analysis of Brett's treatment of Joe, see the comments following the second presentation of Brett's Story, in Chapter 25.)

Note to Brett's Story: Power-Seeking Students

Power-seeking students challenge the teacher's authority in order to gain acceptance from their peers. If the teacher effects compliance, the advantage, therefore, is only temporary. The power struggle intensifies, and the teacher–student relationship deteriorates.

- Dreikurs, R., Grundwald, B., & Pepper, F. (1982). *Maintaining sanity in the classroom: Classroom management techniques* (2nd ed.). New York: Harper & Row.
- Levin, J., & Shanken-Kaye, J. (2002). *From disrupter to achiever: Creating successful learning environments for the self-control classroom.* Dubuque, IA: Kendall/Hunt.

On the other hand, Kohn (2006a) would argue that power-seeking students might be reacting sensibly to their being powerless.

- Kohn, A. (2006a). *Beyond discipline: From compliance to community, 10th anniversary edition.* Alexandria, VA: Association for Supervision and Curriculum Development.

Andrea's Story

During the previous week, I introduced three new concepts through three different activities. I was concerned that the students had experienced overload and would need more time to finish their projects and understand the concepts. So I decided to use the next class as a "work" period. I envisioned students welcoming this additional time.

I informed the students that during this lesson, they were to finish their projects. I did not provide a structure or time frame. I merely told them of this incredible opportunity to complete their work.

I couldn't understand why they didn't jump at the chance. But the truth hit hard when one girl, who was becoming quite proficient at

(Continued)

(Continued)

writing her name in bubble letters, said to me, "You just couldn't think of anything else for us to do." I couldn't have said it better myself. Although I truly believed that the students needed more time to understand the concepts, I should have provided a structure for this to happen. I just didn't invest enough effort in planning.

Unstructured time generates boredom, restlessness, and disruption. Instead of blaming her students for rejecting the "incredible opportunity" she had given them, Andrea, unlike Brett, saw herself as responsible for the failure to plan, a perspective that gave her the power to prevent such failures in the future. *Only when you recognize your own contribution to a problem do you have any power to solve it*.

Andrea needed to create a lesson, aside from the project, to assess and enhance her students' understandings of the three concepts. For example, she could start such a lesson with the following **do-now:** For the three concepts, make a list of terms you associate with each one's meaning.

Then she could have her students work in pairs. Assigning one-third of the pairs to each concept, she could have each pair, with the additional support of books and notes, make a concept map on a transparency using as many terms from the two lists that the pair could agree to include. Thoughtful questions usually emerge during this kind of activity.

Next, she could ask to have a few maps of each concept projected. Each pair would explain the meanings embedded in its map, while she invited the others to compare their understandings with those displayed, another opportunity for thoughtful questions to emerge.

For closure, she could have each student write an answer to this question: How has your understanding of each of the three concepts changed during this lesson? Time permitting, she could elicit some responses orally.

How could you create a lesson to assess and enhance your students' understanding of some concepts?

Note to Andrea's Story: Concept Mapping

Novak and Gowin (1984) and Novak (1998) explain how concept mapping can be used as a learning and assessment tool for students (and teachers) at every grade level and for every subject. The mapmaker creates a hierarchical display of concepts while precisely and concisely identifying the relationships among them.

- Novak, J. D. (1998). *Learning, creating, and using knowledge: Concept maps as facilitative tools in schools and corporations.* Mahwah, NJ: Erlbaum.
- Novak, J. D., & Gowin, D. B. (1984). *Learning how to learn.* New York: Cambridge University Press.

INADEQUATE PLANNING
FOR THE EXECUTION OF A LESSON

Michael's Story

One of my first lessons was memorable because I made mistakes that could have been prevented if I had taken a little more time to plan. The lesson was a review to prepare the students for their mid-term exam. Before the review was to begin, I was going to collect the book reports that were due that day. I was also going to return their graded book reports. The first mistake I made was not waiting for everyone to be seated before explaining my plan for the day.

I began the class by choosing two students to return the graded book reports and asking the entire class to pass up those that were due. Many of the students were either just coming into the room or otherwise out of their seats when I started doing this. As a result, the two students I had picked to pass out the reports were bumping into those who hadn't yet taken their seats. Furthermore, the students who arrived later didn't hear my announcement about handing in the report that was due. So I ended up having to repeat myself.

After these administrative details were out of the way, I began the review. The review went pretty well, but I hadn't explained what was expected of them and how much time they would have to complete their task. And because of the time I'd wasted at the very beginning, I couldn't give them the time they needed to finish.

(Continued)

(Continued)

Now I wait until everyone is seated, signal that it's time to begin, and then say what I expect of them for that period. This way no one is confused. Everyone knows what to do. A few students will always come late or not listen to or remember all the directions, so I display a telegraphed version of the plan on a transparency. I have come to realize that good classroom management comes from planning the "how" as well as the "what" of a lesson.

Michael highlights the importance of planning for the execution as well as the content of a lesson and then communicating that plan to his students.

Michelle's Story

I decided to play *Jeopardy!* with my students so they could review the material and earn some extra points for the exam. I thought I had planned the game extremely well, but when I tried it, it flopped. A lot of things went wrong. First, I thought I could handle being the host, questioner, scorekeeper, and judge of which group had "buzzed in" first, but it was impossible for one person to take on all these roles. Second, the students were confused about the rules. Maybe I should have stopped the game and done something else.

But I really liked the idea of playing a game as a review. The kids liked the idea too. So when it came time to review for the next exam, I decided to do things differently. The day before the game, I printed up a set of directions for the students to read over and discuss. I also chose three volunteers, one for each of the following jobs: to keep a tally of the scores, to determine which group had buzzed in first, and to erase the categories already selected. Some kids were confused in the beginning but fewer than during the previous game. Now, every time we play the game, they get better and better with the procedure.

The important thing I learned is that you might never be able to predict all the trouble spots. Just see what works and what doesn't, and go from there. You can't give up immediately.

Michelle, like Michael, realized the need to plan for the execution of her lesson. However, she gave her students additional opportunities to learn the procedure, in this case the **routine** for playing *Jeopardy!* so she could better execute that kind of lesson in the future. A routine is a set of procedures (with implicit behavioral expectations) to execute a particular activity. *If used consistently, a routine minimizes the time and energy needed to direct a regular classroom event.* Accordingly, routines are well worth teaching early in the school year. How could you use a routine to enhance the execution of one of your lessons?

When Your Lesson Is Boring

Boring lessons generate inattentiveness, indifference, and ultimately hostility. Two teachers realized their lessons were boring, made a change, and enjoyed the added benefit of a better relationship with their students. On the other hand, a third teacher had an activity he thought would be boring. Instead it turned out to be exciting. Why was his activity exciting?

Marty's Story

The topic in my honors class was basic chemistry. The lecture portion was about atoms, elements, and the Periodic Table. Then I planned to give the students a puzzle to become familiar with using the table.

I had been feeling frustrated. I wanted to have more rapport with my students and break free from the monotony of my lessons. I had gotten to the point of explaining the diatomic elements. The mnemonic I used was HOFBrINCl. The presentation was becoming deadly, to my mind soporific. The time had come for a change.

I went to the board and drew a picture of "Dr. HOFBrINCl." It took a few beats for the students to get the gag. Then the class started laughing. The next thing I knew, they were criticizing the poor doctor—his eyes were too beady—and they gave him glasses and a bit of a face-lift. It was a breath of fresh air. Everyone relaxed. The atmosphere since then has become more spontaneous; our interactions, more genuine.

Marty took the risk of using his sense of humor to enliven his lesson. *Humor defuses tension and promotes a positive relationship with students but only when directed at the teacher or a situation, never at a student.*

Note to Marty's Story: Humor in the Classroom

Saphier and Gower (1982) explain the benefits of humor in the classroom. Humor defuses tension, and as a shared experience, it promotes a sense of community.

- Saphier, J., & Gower, R. (1982). *The skillful teacher.* Carlisle, MA: Research for Better Teaching.

Levin and Nolan (2007) make the distinction between humor, which is directed at the teacher or situation, and sarcasm, which is directed at a student or students. Likewise, Ginott (1972) warns that sarcasm destroys the teacher–student relationship.

- Ginott, H. G. (1972). *Teacher and child: A book for parents and teachers.* New York: Macmillan.
- Levin, J., & Nolan, J. F. (2007). *Principles of classroom management: A professional decision-making model* (5th ed.). Boston: Allyn & Bacon.

Peter's Story

I was giving my earth science class some notes on weathering and erosion in preparation for their final exam. Many students started to complain about too many lessons with too many notes. So I went out into the field and made a videotape of the Kaaterskill Creek to show them an example of weathering and erosion. Making the video was

(Continued)

(Continued)

good because the students got a familiar reference for the concepts and saw that I cared about them. I learned that if students see their teacher doing something extra for them, then more times than not, they'll appreciate it and try to learn the material.

Instead of blaming his students for complaining, Peter accepted the responsibility for making his lessons interesting. He boosted his students' interest by demonstrating the concepts of weathering and erosion with a local example. More generally, he attended to his students' feelings and responded graciously to them. *Welcome the expression of your students' feelings as feedback to improve your teaching.*

How do you think Ryan, Jill, or Henry (Chapter 1) might have enlivened Marty's or Peter's lesson?

One way Marty or Peter might have enlivened his own lesson could have been by punctuating his lectures with opportunities for his students to wrestle with the concepts themselves. For example, as soon as Marty introduced the diatomic elements (H, O, F, Br, I, N, and Cl), he could have asked them to take a few minutes, perhaps with the help of their book, the Periodic Table, and a partner, to determine why those elements would be diatomic. Similarly, Peter could have asked his students to make a chart to show how weathering and erosion compare. *Punctuating a lecture with thought-provoking questions (typically "why," "how," or "what if" questions) can stimulate interest.* Trivial questions, however, especially the rapid stream of "what" questions associated with a **recitation,** compound boredom (see John's Story, Chapter 8).

Note to Marty's and Peter's Stories: Alleviating Boredom

To alleviate boredom, Good and Weinstein (1986) recommend that teachers have their students practice using the concepts during the lesson in cognitively active and meaningful ways.

- Good, T. L., & Weinstein, R. (1986). Teacher expectations: A framework for exploring classrooms. In K. K. Zumwalt (Ed.), *Improving teaching* (The 1986 ASCD Yearbook, pp. 63–86). Alexandria, VA: Association for Supervision and Curriculum Development.

Joe's Story

It was during the middle of the week that a certain event surprised and impressed me. It was after lunch, and I had my problematic sixth-period biology class. This class consists of sophomores, juniors, and seniors, all low achievers. Most of my classroom management challenges come from this class. At times, I have found myself dreading their arrival, afraid of their reaction to my activities. But on this occasion, they delighted me.

I was introducing them to the different kinds of cells and planned to have them first list as many body parts as they could. Then I could relate each body part to its various kinds of cells.

I anticipated a hesitant group that would come up with only a few body parts at best, but these students loved the activity. Before I knew it, the activity had kindled a competition with questions emerging from previously unresponsive students: "Can we use internal and external parts?" "Do hair and fingernails count?" These students were excited! They took an activity I thought would be boring, one that would seem trivial, and turned it into the basis for learning about the different kinds of cells.

Joe's activity generated excitement because, far from being trivial, its level of difficulty was appropriate for his students. Accordingly, they believed they could be successful, so successful that they spontaneously competed with one another. Second, the activity related to his students' everyday knowledge, in this case of their own body. Just as Peter used his students' everyday knowledge of the Kaaterskill Creek to help them appreciate weathering and erosion, Joe used his students' everyday knowledge of their own body to help them appreciate the different kinds of cells. *Students appreciate learning about a concept they can relate to everyday life.* How could you relate a concept you teach to your students' everyday life?

When Your Directions Generate Frustration

The first four **stories** in this chapter are about a **novice teacher**'s directions generating frustration and disorder. In the first of the four, the method of delivering the directions generates the students' frustration. In the next three, the fault is with the directions themselves. The fifth story, however, is different. It raises this question: How can a novice teacher determine whether the students' frustration is genuine or just a ruse to impede the progress of the lesson?

THE DELIVERY

Melissa's Story

The activity for the lesson was to make a moon wheel to demonstrate the cycle of the moon's phases. A number of materials and several steps were involved in making the wheel. Each student was to cut out various pieces of paper and then glue one of them to a piece of cardboard. The other pieces of paper were then to be placed on top of the cardboard and fastened so each could rotate. The materials for each step were handed out when the entire class was ready for that step. The directions for that step were then given orally.

Unfortunately, I had enough scissors for only about half the students. Also, I didn't allow the students to glue their own projects. Instead, I walked around the room and glued the paper for them.

The students were especially rowdy. They were not paying attention to the directions. Once they finished the given step, they would begin talking with their neighbor. It was difficult to regain their attention to give them the directions for the next step. Also, many students had lost the notes they needed to identify each phase on the wheel. Students ended up sharing their notes, which gave them even more opportunities to be rowdy.

Now I print a complete set of directions so everyone can work without having to wait for others. And I print any additional notes they might need, not for them to keep but to have as a reference during class. I also have students work in pairs, even for individual projects, so they can share materials and help each other before having to ask me for help. And when they are in pairs, I can get around to them more efficiently.

Melissa's manner of delivering the directions failed to take into account the different rates at which her students would be working, that virtually all of them would end up having to wait at some point, probably several times in addition to having to wait for a pair of scissors and then again for her to glue their paper. First, she had too much **dead time,** the time during a lesson when students are not engaged in a learning activity. *Dead time generates disorder.*

Second, she delivered the directions only orally. To attend to her directions, everyone in the entire class would have to be quiet at the same time and for an extended period of time, an unrealistic expectation during project work, and the students would have to understand, remember, and be able to follow the directions upon hearing them, another unrealistic expectation. *Students need a set of written directions.* By printing the directions, she eliminates the dead time from a piecemeal delivery, and by having her students work in pairs, she reduces the dead time when they need help.

Third, the cognitive burden of constructing the wheel probably precluded her students' understanding the principle behind it, namely, why the moon has phases, presumably the point of the lesson. In short, Melissa's students may have executed the procedure without understanding its meaning. *Difficult tasks perceived as meaningless generate frustration and consequently disorder.* Melissa might, therefore, improve her lesson further by providing partly or wholly constructed wheels and focusing instead on her students using the wheel to identify, justify, and predict the moon's phases. *Hands-on is not enough; the task also has to be brains-on.* How could you reduce your students' cognitive burden so as to make a task more brains-on?

THE DIRECTIONS THEMSELVES

In the first two stories that follow, the teacher devises a way to forestall her students' frustration. The third story is about a novice teacher who needs a more promising solution than threatening to punish the entire class.

Charlotte's Story

Here's why everything went wrong. The directions were so confusing (e.g., missing steps, unfamiliar terms) that even I had trouble figuring out what to do. I didn't want to give my ninth graders this editing activity as it was written, but it was a standard activity for our English Department and had already been printed. The department is charged for each copy, so it's cheap about printing revisions.

I spent almost the entire time explaining the directions, which generated even more questions, a million and one to be exact. So a million and one questions later, it seemed as if we were ready to begin. We formed groups, the troublemakers swearing they would work on the task maturely.

Then I saw two students blatantly copying from each other. To be honest, I myself would have been tempted. The directions were just so confusing. What to do? They knew I had seen them copying, so, of course, I had to take their papers away. But what could I give them to do instead?

More questions from other groups! So many that I forgot about the copiers, now with nothing to do, distracting those who were trying to do the task. The scene looked so weird, it was almost funny. As I remember it, the troublemakers were standing in the back left corner of the room, some of the others having drifted over to them, while the copiers were attracting another group in the back right corner.

Now I simplify directions. If I can't give each student (or even each pair) a copy of simplified directions, then I at least summarize the essentials on a transparency and project them. This additional preparation is well worth the effort!

Charlotte's students, like Melissa's, probably experienced cognitive overload just trying to interpret the directions and thus missed the meaning of the activity, experienced frustration, and became disorderly. Charlotte recognized and has overcome this problem by having ready a set of simpler directions. She did not, however, focus on the problem of her students copying. How would you have treated their copying?

Their copying may have been the result of a genuine attempt to make sense of the activity. I wonder what they would have said if, instead of taking their papers, she had asked, "I see you're having trouble with this activity. What help do you need to be able to do it?" Instead of punishing, *a "working with" rather than a "doing to" approach promotes student maturity.*

Note to Melissa's and Charlotte's Stories: Time on Task

Students will spend more time on task if given both oral and written directions.

- Brophy, J. E. (1988). Educating teachers about managing classrooms and students. *Teaching and Teacher Education, 4,* 1–18.

Barbara's Story

After completing the lab on density, the students had to create a graph and answer a few questions. I demonstrated how to set up the graph with a title and labels for the x- and y-axes. As I circulated around the room, however, I discovered that a couple of groups needed help devising the scale for each axis. After attending to these two groups, I realized the rest of the class was getting antsy because they too didn't know how to devise a scale. I simply hadn't given them enough instruction. I should have known better. I had experienced this many times before, kids having more trouble with a set of directions than I expected. Now I had to recapture their attention and instruct them on how to set up the scales for their graph.

I wasted 20 minutes of the lesson before I could get all the groups ready to make their graphs. Now I check for students' background knowledge and comprehension along the way before I get too far into a set of directions.

Like many novice teachers, Barbara overestimated her students' background knowledge. Now she knows to *check for understanding frequently and be ready to explain the basics.*

Tara's Story

I planned a hands-on activity for my two earth science classes. The purpose of the lesson was for them to learn how two different kinds of fossils, molds and casts, form. I planned to have the students make both molds and casts using clay, sea shells, and play dough. First, I divided the class into six groups of about four, asked them to read the section in their textbook on molds and casts, and gave them a handout with some general directions. But I purposely did not tell them how to use the materials. I wanted them to figure out each process for themselves.

The first class went well. The students examined the materials and, with only a few pointers to the information in the textbook, were able to make their samples. Then as a class, we discussed how they figured out what to do with the materials and solve the problems they encountered. After the discussion, they placed their samples in a box, returned to their group, and examined the samples made by another group. They then had to determine whether each sample was a mold or a cast and justify their conclusion in writing. The class went well. They understood the differences between a mold and a cast and how each was formed. And they enjoyed themselves.

The second class, however, was a complete disaster. The students began by complaining about their group assignment. That should have clued me in. I circulated about the room as I had done with the first class but found that several groups couldn't figure out the directions and felt lost. So I reminded them to read the textbook. I had to speak to one particular student several times about his behavior. He was misusing the clay and play dough and breaking the shells. After taking care of that problem, I believed everything would run smoothly, that is, until I realized that time was running out.

To continue the lesson as planned, I had to collect the samples whether the students had finished them or not. At this point, I thought they would be willing if not eager to discuss the problems they had encountered. Wrong! Almost no one participated. So we proceeded to the next segment of the lesson, when they were to identify another group's samples.

The nightmare began quickly. The class became uncontrollable. Several of the students were breaking the samples and throwing the pieces at each other. I addressed the entire class and told them they must control themselves and that if this behavior continued, we could no longer work in groups or do any hands-on tasks.

Tara failed to adapt the directions to her second class, even after realizing her students could not follow them. Moreover, because she blamed her students instead of recognizing her own contribution to their frustration, she could not remedy the situation. *Only when you recognize your own contribution to a problem do you have any power to solve it.*

Instead, she threatened to punish the entire class. Punishing the entire class for the **misbehavior** of several is patently unfair. *Never impose group punishment.* Tara forfeited any claim to being the moral authority by threatening to impose an unfair punishment. Besides, *punishment does not deter misbehavior; it fosters resentment, not cooperation.* Second, *using threats (or bribes) to control student behavior undermines any potential for a mutually respectful relationship.* Students see threats (and bribes) as the teacher's attempt to manipulate them.

Beginning with the first signs, how could Tara have either prevented or checked the disorder?

A Ruse?

Susan's Story

The event occurred during my seventh-period French class. I was giving directions for an in-class activity, each student to draw a scene from *Le Misanthrope* and then write a summary in French of what was happening in that scene. I had already presented the lesson to three earlier classes that day. The lesson had gone well so I didn't anticipate any problems.

Following the **do-now,** I started to introduce the activity, giving the directions as I had done for the previous classes. Several students, however, repeatedly raised their hands claiming not to understand the activity even before I had finished explaining it. It was taking twice as long to deliver the directions to this class, and I was getting frustrated trying to get them to understand. By the time I distributed the materials, they had only a short time for the activity. As I reflected on this lesson, I was disappointed in myself because I had allowed a few students to slow down the lesson intentionally.

How can a novice teacher determine whether the students' questions are genuine or just a ruse to impede the progress of the lesson? Inasmuch as Susan's directions were effective in her three earlier classes, her first step was to look at the students who were generating the questions. Had they a history of being obstructionists?

Regardless of their intentions, however, *whenever you have some students monopolizing the class's time, you need to decentralize instruction.* Susan needed to stop the questions, assign her students to their groups, and invite them to help each other, perhaps asking each group to first list the essential steps of the procedure. Circulating among the groups to see who needed help, checking first on the ones who had had questions, she would then deliver the materials to each group only upon its demonstrating an understanding of the procedure.

Note to Susan's Story: Teacher Expectations

Students, especially but not only low-ability students (see John's Story, Chapter 8), know how to distract their teachers from the learning objective, slow down the pace of the lesson or otherwise impede its progress, and press their teachers to lower their expectations so they have to learn less of the curriculum.

- Bullough, R. V., Jr. (1989). *First-year teacher: A case study.* New York: Teachers College Press.
- Evertson, C. (1982). Differences in instructional activities in higher- and lower-achieving junior high English and math classes. *Elementary School Journal, 82,* 329–350.

5

When the Activities You've Planned Don't Fill the Allotted Time

The only thing worse than a lesson that's too long is one that's too short. Both are regrettable, but management problems erupt when the activities you've planned don't fill the allotted time. Here are five **novice teachers' stories** about how each encountered, overcame, or learned to avert an under-planned lesson.

Heidi's Story

The problem came at the end of the lesson. It has been a rule since the beginning of the year that the students are to stay in their seats until the bell rings. After the lesson was over, 2 minutes were left until the end of the period. The students began packing up and walking around as soon as they realized the lesson had ended. They also started getting loud.

I attempted to get the students seated again, but I could not be heard over the noise. So I shouted. Some of the students found this funny. I am such a quiet, calm person that, I suppose, it amused them to see me get frustrated. Consequently, I spent the last 2 minutes quieting and settling the students.

Even a veteran teacher cannot pace every lesson precisely. Heidi was not prepared to extend her lesson. Later, she devised a solution based on an essential principle of **classroom management:** *Teachers cannot control their students' behaviors, although they can influence and react to them. Teachers can, however, control their own behavior.* Heidi began to prepare extra work for each lesson in case she finished sooner than expected.

Dawes's Story

In my rush to get to school on time, I forgot to bring a copy of my lesson plan with the sheet for the activity that was to serve as both the assessment of student learning and summary for the lesson. I realized this fact about two-thirds of the way to school. In the last minutes of the drive, though, I got an idea. During the first period, I would see how much time the lesson took without the sheet, figure out something to fill that time, and then use that plan for the rest of the classes.

The first class went pretty well. The students used the extra 10 minutes to organize their assignments for the rest of the day. Thinking this was the solution to my problem, I suggested that the third-period class do the same thing. It was not a solution, however, and I was caught off guard when they used the free time to socialize, fool around, and try to sneak out of the room before the bell rang. I had overlooked the fact that unlike the first-period class, the third-period class would not be shaking off the cloak of sleep.

Unlike Heidi, Dawes expected the shortfall but failed to plan adequately for it. He came to realize that *the teacher needs to have a definite plan for every activity.*

Chad's Story

It's a B-day, and I have the students for almost 2 hours. Yes, block scheduling gives you long periods of time with your students. This allows me to put together great lengthy lesson plans that engage them in group activities. But what happens when you finish your activities and you still have about 50 minutes of class time left?

Was I unprepared for class? Wasn't my jigsaw/expert group/concept map/group work enough? All was going great until I looked up at the clock and realized I still had about 50 minutes of class time remaining. I started to pace the room to jog my brain to generate ideas about how to keep them busy for another 50 minutes. Well, soon they all started to filter back to their assigned seats, and I was frantically trying to come up with a follow-up activity. My so-called great lesson would quickly become a disaster if I didn't come up with something fast. As I glanced around the room, my eyes fell upon the video collection in the back cabinet. I'm a genius. I'll show a video. What a great idea! Thank heavens for VCRs and TVs.

Chad, like Heidi, did not expect the shortfall, but in his case, it was substantial, due to errors more in the planning than the execution of his lesson. No novice can predict the amount of time an activity in a given class will take, but *when class periods are longer, timing errors compound.*

For those substantial timing errors (or when administrators have to extend a class period, sometimes indefinitely), you need something more strategic than a collection of videos. You need an appealing activity, one you could adapt to any time frame and realize with little or no preparation and few materials, regardless of the day's topic. Have the students create something from an imaginative point of view! It could be a story, poster, skit, song, TV commercial, newspaper article, or even a filmstrip about the topic.

I remember visiting a student biology teacher in a New York City public high school. Her topic for the day was the female reproductive system. Having planned the activity for a 40-minute lesson, she could just as easily have expanded it to fit a longer time frame. She divided her students into groups, gave them 20 minutes, and challenged each group to come up with a 2-minute presentation to explain the function of any part of the female reproductive system. She provided her students with nothing more than the ordinary materials you would expect to find in a classroom: textbooks, markers, poster paper, composition paper, drawing paper, pencils, and erasers. Twenty minutes later, everyone was eager to see the presentations.

I shall never forget one presentation, a skit from the point of view of an ovum. Here was a 16-year-old boy doing repeated somersaults across the room while his partners took turns reading their script to explain the journey of an ovum from the ovary, through the Fallopian tube, to the uterus. Similarly, Chad's having his students create an imaginative interpretation of some aspect of his topic could have, with little or no preparation and few materials, productively engaged his students for another 15 to 50 minutes.

Luz's Story

At the end of one of my lessons, I realized we still had about 7 minutes left in the period. I told the students to stay in their seats until the bell rang. First the students began to talk. Then the volume increased. In the back of the room, a couple of boys began to play fight. Nothing got out of control, but I had to redirect the students, and that made me uncomfortable.

I made some changes for my next presentation of that lesson. First, I slowed my pace through the lecture and gave more examples. Then I added some activities. I also created a safety pack of transparencies. Now, whenever I have time at the end of a lesson, I pull them out and we look at them. On some of them, I have multiple-choice questions to review material we've already covered. On others, we enjoy *The Far Side* cartoons for a laugh.

Chad happened upon a onetime solution. Luz, on the other hand, created a tool for a more lasting solution, a safety pack of transparencies. Alternatively, she could have had her students write a one- or two-sentence response to their choice of one of the following questions: "What was this lesson about?" "What did you come to know today?" "How is this topic important to you?" and "What questions do you still have?" As time permits, she could then have students read or tell about their own response or comment on another's. In either case, she would have an instructional segment appropriate to append to any lesson, one flexible in length and requiring no significant preparation. How would you plan for such a segment?

Lisa's Story

My biology class is made up of mostly ninth graders. They are usually a difficult group to keep on task. They meet eighth or ninth period every day and sometimes come from gym class. We were studying the human respiratory system, and I had planned an activity where the kids would have to construct a working model of the lungs. Once each group had constructed its model, the students were to show it to me and then work in their group on some questions. The management problem arose when some groups finished their model and questions well before the others. They then proceeded to poke, push, and bother each other and distract those who were not yet finished. Asking them to sit quietly was simply not working.

The problem arose because I had not given them enough work. Students should not have idle time. Now, in order to accommodate those who work more quickly, I make sure to include enrichment work along with the essential tasks. The fastest groups continue to work, and I stop the activity as soon as the slowest group has finished the essentials.

Lisa's management problem was different from the others, who each had extra time at the end of their lesson. She had students with spare time in the middle of the lesson as they waited for others to finish. In her search for a solution, Lisa realized that *everyone need not complete every learning task, just its essential parts.*

Luz and Lisa each developed a strategy for engaging or keeping their students engaged in a learning activity. Luz developed a ready-made, generally appropriate supplementary activity for lesson closure, whereas Lisa assigned enrichment work for all individual and group activities. As a result, Luz and Lisa each demonstrated that *a novice teacher can avert the **discipline problems** consequential to all but the most egregious planning shortfalls.*

Note to Luz's and Lisa's Stories: Overplanning

Kerrie, the first-year teacher in Bullough's book, explained that her overplanning improved her classroom management. "I'd rather bombard them than let them bombard me with their free time" (p. 39).

- Bullough, R. V., Jr. (1989). *First-year teacher: A case study.* New York: Teachers College Press.

Getting the Class Settled for the Start of the Lesson

Getting the class settled for the start of a lesson can be an ordeal, especially for afternoon classes, when students are restless and easily distracted. Here are the **stories** of three **novice teachers** and the **routine** they each used to start especially an afternoon lesson smoothly.

Anne's Story

I must confess that I have broken every rule on **classroom management**! Fortunately, I have paid dearly for every error, making each one a learning experience.

For example, the **do-now:** Initially, I used it faithfully and enthusiastically. Yet somehow my intentions went awry until my students started asking, "What does 'do-now' mean?" I was backed up with undone lesson plans and I was (and still am) panicking for in-class activities, never mind trying to find or create a do-now.

Guess what? I am back on the wagon. It's well worth the effort to start the class off with a routine to transition into the lesson calmly.

Anne felt the pressure to come up with a novel do-now for each lesson. The charm of the do-now, however, is in its regularity. It need not be a novel activity, merely an easy one, preferably about the previous or upcoming lesson, something the students can do independently for a few minutes. But *the do-now must be an activity that requires students to sit down and take out their notebook, perhaps their textbook, and a pencil or pen.*

Mark's Story

The times during class when I would have the most trouble were at the start of each lesson and whenever I would ask the students to take out a book, calculator, or their homework. These times seemed to be equivalent to my saying, "Feel free to discuss your weekend plans with your friends."

But then I came up with a single solution to both problems. I began to use a two-part do-now. First, I give them a list of vocabulary words for that day's lesson and they use their textbook to write a definition for each word. Second, I give them a list of the materials they'll need to have ready for the lesson.

This expanded do-now has helped me in a few ways. First, it gets the students involved in quiet seatwork as soon as they enter the classroom. Second, they are not repeatedly creating a disturbance rummaging through their backpacks. All their materials are at hand right from the start. Third, I can see that when they start gathering their materials, they are finished with their vocabulary words. Then I know it's almost time for me to begin.

Mark used the same kind of do-now for every lesson. Some teachers regularly use a set of vocabulary words, either to unscramble or spot in a computer-generated word-find puzzle. Then the students write the definition of each word using their textbook as a reference. Other teachers generate a set of multiple-choice questions to review the previous lesson. After choosing an answer, the students then write a justification for their answer. *No matter what 3- to 5-minute activity or activities you regularly use for your do-now, your students should be able to find the written directions themselves, in the same place every day, as they enter your classroom.* What kinds of do-now activities could you make up?

Jodi's Story

It was difficult to quiet down my afternoon class to a level low enough for me to start. For about a week, I would shout over the energized chatterboxes. Yes, I gained their attention, but I didn't feel that the method was working. My energy was being wasted along with the class's time. Anyway, it seemed as if I never stopped battling the noise. So I decided to use a technique I learned in my Methods of Teaching class. I would stand boldly and silently before the class. I recalled learning from that class that they would notice me and nudge one another to shush so I could begin.

The first day, I was pleased with the results. But the following day, some students in the front row used this time to ask me questions like "Will you check the homework?" and "When will we have a test?" I took this time to answer their questions and then wondered why the Silence Signal wasn't working.

Later that week, I observed another teacher using this signal. She was successful, I saw, because she ignored all questions until she had absolute silence. So I tried again, this time ignoring the front row. Since then, I have found the Silence Signal to be a wonderful way to start each lesson and conserve my much-needed energy.

Jodi learned that *everyone needs to be quiet for the Silence Signal to work,* especially the teacher, who must model the expected behavior. Jodi also tells us that she stood boldly before the class. *Teachers can strengthen a signal with multiple cues,* a bold stance but also a resolute expression and a gesture, such as folded arms or an index finger across the lips, using that set of cues consistently with and exclusively for that signal.

Note to Jodi's Story:
Teachers Abiding by Their Own Rules

Jodi's students heeded her Silence Signal only when she herself abided by it. In fact, teachers failing to abide by their own rules exacerbate disruptive behaviors because the students come to distrust those teachers, seeing them as disingenuous, as people who want only to manipulate them.

- French, J. R. P., & Raven, B. (1960). The bases of social power. In D. Cartwright & A. Zander (Eds.), *Group dynamics: Research and theory* (2nd ed., pp. 607–623). Evanston, IL: Row-Peterson.

Each of the three teachers adopted a routine to start or signal the start of each lesson. *If used consistently, a routine minimizes the time and energy needed to direct a regular classroom event.* A routine also reduces the number of decisions the teacher must make. However, teachers need to teach their students the routine explicitly, use it consistently, and encourage their students to learn it. Consider using both routines, the do-now and the Silence Signal, to start your lessons. Use Mark's do-now so that students come in, sit down, and, without prompting, get ready for the lesson. Then use Jodi's signal to start the lesson as they're gathering the last of their materials.

7

When You Have a Persistently Noisy Class

Do you see yourself as a **classroom manager** or as only a **disciplinarian**? A disciplinarian concentrates on treating **misbehavior,** whereas a classroom manager concentrates on continuing the lesson so as to engage as many students as possible in learning activities. The distinction is important. In this chapter, the degree of success of the **novice teachers** coping with a persistently noisy class depended upon their ability to conceptualize their role more broadly than that of a disciplinarian, to see themselves instead as managers.

Ten novice teachers each contended with unremitting side chatter, usually in an afternoon class. Their **stories** are arranged in sets to demonstrate both within and across the sets the range in the teachers' ability to claim their power as a manager and use that power to curb the noise.

In the first set of stories, two novice teachers each begin redefining themselves as a manager. In the second set, three novice teachers each claim their power to be a manager and then use that power to effect various strategies. In the third set, three novice teachers each begin to formulate a systematic management plan, and in the fourth set, two novice teachers each act to reshape their class's norms.

REDEFINING THEMSELVES AS CLASSROOM MANAGERS

Jenny's Story

During my fourth week of teaching global studies, I confronted my first behavior problem. In my class of 25, I have 6 students who, on any given day, could all be called to the office or even suspended. Five of the six are failing. On this day, by some chance, all six were present.

The disruptions started as soon as the bell rang. Rarely are the offenses major, just a constant stream of minor interruptions: Sean out of his seat every 2 minutes, Jacinta asking what grade she got on her last test, Karen's constant chatter, and CJ playing the drums with his pencil. In addition, on this day the other students were having trouble understanding the lesson and were getting restless as much from the distractions as the material itself.

My own attention was on my lecture, but as my frustration level rose, I began making mistakes and had difficulty explaining the concepts. I found myself raising my voice and pleading with them to sit down, quiet down, and pay attention. In short, I had lost control of the class.

I responded by yelling and singling out Paul, who happened to be the ringleader at the time. I informed him, along with the rest of the class, that he was failing because he hadn't been paying attention and that I was assigning him an afterschool detention to discuss his behavior and missing assignments. Paul responded by informing me that he wasn't going to come and that I couldn't make him do anything. Annoyed and angry, I stupidly persisted with this confrontation. All the while, the other students were hooting and hollering and egging on the circus until, after about 3 minutes, I was literally saved by the bell. All I had accomplished in the entire 42 minutes was to make a fool of myself.

Looking back, I see that I had been under the impression that it was my fault the students were acting out. My job is to teach the lesson and concentrate on the class instead of the disrupters. So I need to work on strategies to advance the lesson and avoid taking their misbehaviors personally and letting them get the best of me.

Instead of singling out Paul, Jenny needed to *address the situation, not the shortcomings of the student(s)*. For example, she could have said to the class, "I get frustrated when the class is so noisy," perhaps even adding, "Let's take a few deep breaths, and then I'll continue."

More fundamentally, Jenny held a misconception common among novice teachers that she is responsible for controlling her students' behaviors. In truth, *teachers cannot control their students' behaviors, although they can influence and react to them. Teachers can, however, control their own behavior.*

As she sheds her misconception, Jenny can define her role more broadly. Instead of being preoccupied as a disciplinarian, she can become a classroom manager devising strategies for preventing rather than merely treating the disruptions. And once she can separate their misbehavior from her sense of worth, she need not take their misbehaviors personally. *Resist the tendency to take your students' misbehaviors personally.*

Patrick's Story

I found myself giving the students various ultimatums in response to their misbehavior. For example, "If you don't stop the chatter, I will lengthen the homework assignment" or "If you don't pay attention, I will give you a quiz." I was bargaining with the students to act appropriately. The students would temporarily direct their attention to me, but after just a few seconds, they would return to their private conversations.

I had forgotten that I was the one in charge, that I didn't have to hand out ultimatums. I simply had to make my expectations clear and then treat the students in accord with those expectations.

Patrick came to realize that he already had the power to manage his class and that he could exercise that power by communicating his expectations. *Novice teachers have difficulty claiming their power as the authority*, some, probably including Patrick, failing to distinguish between being authoritative and authoritarian. As a result, they experience a tension between their conception of an authority as necessarily authoritarian and the image they have of themselves as a warm and caring adult.

In the next set of stories, Thomas, Alison, and Casey claim their power, each going further than Patrick to manage the side chatter.

CLAIMING THEIR AUTHORITY

Thomas's Story

The students had started to get unruly, the noise level getting a little louder each day. My gentle reminders, which worked at first, were no longer effective. It soon dawned on me that although it was against my nature, I would have to get stern with them. So in one class, the worst of them, I started the lesson with a thunderous announcement, one that froze them on the spot:

"Listen up," I shouted. "I am in this class to teach, and you are here to learn, but the noise level is keeping everyone from accomplishing these goals. From now on, if I have to tell anyone twice during the same lesson to quiet down, I will write out a referral and send it to the principal's office. I sincerely mean this and give you my word that I will follow through on this." That happened last week.

So far, except for a few minor disturbances, the students have been comparative angels. I hope I never have to follow through with my threat, but alas, I know I will.

Thomas came to realize that he, like Patrick, must claim his power as the authority in order to establish and maintain an effective learning environment. Although he framed his rule as a threat, Thomas explained to his students that its purpose, far from being arbitrary, was for their benefit. Second, he provided a warning system for his students to learn his limits and control their behavior accordingly. Third, he spelled out the consequence.

Thomas's rule, however, had disadvantages. First, a referral to the principal's office is an extreme reaction to his students being noisy. *An administrative intervention should be reserved for an emergency*, such as for violence or the threat of violence, not for an ordinary situation like continuing side chatter (see Chapter 29 for examples of appropriate occasions for an administrative intervention). Second, the students needed to see that Thomas, not the principal, was in charge of their class. And third, Thomas threatened his students with a punishment. *Punishment does not deter misbehavior; it fosters resentment, not cooperation.* Thomas needed to find a more promising way to manage their persistent chatter as the following two novice teachers in this set of stories did.

Note to Thomas's Story: Punishment and Misbehavior

Punishment does not curb misbehavior beyond temporary compliance. Instead, students learn that inflicting punishment is the prerogative of the one in charge and that by being more circumspect, they can avoid detection.

- Clarizio, H. F. (1980). *Toward positive classroom discipline* (3rd ed.). New York: Wiley.
- Ginott, H. G. (1972). *Teacher and child: A book for parents and teachers.* New York: Macmillan.
- Kohn, A. (2006a). *Beyond discipline: From compliance to community, 10th anniversary edition.* Alexandria, VA: Association for Supervision and Curriculum Development.

Alison's Story

I am currently working with a low-achievement-level class that has been constantly challenging my management skills. In the beginning, I found myself being too lenient with them. I should have established boundaries. This was difficult for me because I was afraid of coming off as the "bad guy."

But I saw that I needed to control their constant talking. So after an especially difficult class, I devised a new seating chart, carefully choosing where each student would sit. I also realized that implementing this new seating arrangement would require exercising my authority and explaining that I was unhappy with their behavior.

I came into class the next day and projected the new seating chart on the screen. I asked the students to move to their new seats immediately. When faced with opposition, I explained how their behavior was unacceptable and hurting their opportunities to learn. My speaking out definitely got their attention.

I felt better about the class after speaking to them because they could see that I meant business, that I wasn't going to tolerate their misbehavior. They no longer sit with their friends and talk all period, and when they chat a little, I am no longer afraid to speak to them firmly.

I have learned that I can be only so nice. They have to respect my authority. So if you're not getting the respect you need, you have to do something to gain your students' respect.

Alison, like Thomas, came to assume her power as the manager, first by explaining how and why her students' behaviors were unacceptable. And like Thomas, she stated the message briefly, without preaching, blaming, or recounting the past. Her strategy, however, is more promising than Thomas's. Rather than making a threat, she changed her students' seats so as to make it easier for them to control their own behavior. *Rather than impose control, foster students' self-control.*

Casey's Story

My eighth-period class is the most challenging of all. The lessons are typically disrupted by constant chatter and frequent bathroom breaks, all leading to confusion, the need to repeat directions, and the loss of valuable time. This class is always behind my others. I've asked the students to be quiet, taken away their bathroom privileges, and threatened to change their seats. Nothing has worked. I needed to do something else to establish order.

(Continued)

(Continued)

I took control. First, I made a seating chart. The students were shocked that I would actually follow through with my threat to change their seats. Still, I knew that just changing their seats would not be enough. They would soon be comfortable in their new seats, and the disruptions would begin all over again.

So I also made a commitment to provide an activity for them, to settle them down as soon as they entered the classroom. I started preparing a daily **do-now.** Since these two changes, the students have been more attentive, and distractions are few.

Casey too found that her pleas, empty threats, and punishments were useless. She needed to be a manager instead of a disciplinarian. Like Alison, she exercised her newly claimed power by imposing a seating chart. In addition, she instituted a daily **routine,** the do-now, to structure the beginning of each lesson. *The do-now must be an activity that requires students to sit down and take out their notebook, perhaps their textbook, and a pencil or pen.* Once she saw herself as a manager, Casey could create a **proactive management strategy** such as the do-now.

Toward a Systematic Management Plan

Leah's Story

The persistent goal of my seventh-period beauties seemed to be to test my willingness to tolerate distractions. This class is a hyperactive, bright, and social bunch of 35 busy bees who love to talk, talk, talk. How to manage these wild wonders became my 3:00 a.m. obsession. So, yes, I have had a lot of experience with trial and error, and, yes, with failure as well. I found out quickly that asking certain kids nicely to please stop talking was totally ineffective and that I would need other ways of dealing with them.

Veterans advised me that I couldn't just be nice to them, that I would have to be a dictator. Well, that's just not who I am. How could I still be nice without having to tolerate their constant disruptions? I wrestled with this question for an entire weekend. Here's what I decided to do:

First, I changed their seats. Too many yakkers were sitting together. Second, I worked to reduce the **dead time** by preparing and organizing the lesson better. Students just wouldn't have time to yak. Third, I planned more active learning opportunities, using their hyperactivity to my advantage. I have them working in groups since they love to flap their jaws.

Yes, I still lose my patience with them. That will be the case no matter how long I teach, but I don't have to be mean or raise my voice to reduce the number of distractions and get them to cooperate.

First, Leah realized that she had to be comfortable with her management plan. Only then could she uphold it consistently. Second, like Casey, she saw that she could use lesson planning to promote her management as well as her curricular goals. *A teacher needs to consider both management and curricular objectives when planning and executing a lesson.* In particular, she focused on reducing the dead time. *Dead time generates disorder.* So Leah might assign her students a 2-minute task while she is setting up, collecting, or putting away equipment or materials. She could have them individually write a summary of a video they had just seen or have them confer in pairs to compose a statement of their shared understanding of the previous learning activity. How could you reduce some of the dead time in your lessons?

Dina's Story

I came to learn that ninth period, the last period of the day, would be noisier than the others, especially on a Friday. This past Friday, I completed a 5-minute review of the week's lessons, did a 10-minute PowerPoint lecture on the six simple machines and their parts, and then distributed a worksheet that involved the students working in pairs to identify the simple machines and label their parts.

(Continued)

(Continued)

The students were fine in the beginning, but by the time we were ready to go over the worksheet, they were unruly and getting out of their seats.

Looking back, I realize I should have done a few things differently. For one, I should have directed my requests for quiet at the offenders instead of the entire class, and I should have directed them sooner. And I should have realized that the PowerPoint lecture was too passive an activity on a Friday afternoon. I now have more active lessons for Friday afternoons and use little techniques, like "giving the look" when someone first gets a little out of control. That's a lot easier than having to get the whole class back on track, because disorder spreads like a California wildfire.

Like Casey and Leah, Dina's instructional decisions came to be based on management as well as curricular considerations. Also, she began to use a more immediate but less intrusive signal, a nonverbal warning directed at the misbehaver. *Nonverbal signals are better than verbal signals because they do not provoke defensive arguments or hostile confrontations. Nonverbal signals also do not interrupt the flow of the lesson, and they invite the students to control their own behavior.* Perhaps most important, rather than having to improvise under pressure, she began to plan deliberately for the inevitable Friday afternoons.

Dina decided to replace her PowerPoint lecture with her students creating and presenting their own slides. She would divide the class into six groups, one for each simple machine, and have each group create two transparencies, one featuring the parts of its simple machine and the other featuring examples from everyday life. Keeping her initial 5-minute review of the week's lessons, she would then use about 15 minutes for her students to create the transparencies, 15 minutes for their presenting them, and 5 minutes for summarizing and assessing the lesson with the worksheet.

How would you transform a passive lesson into an active one?

Note to Dina's Story: Nonverbal Interventions

For a discussion of nonverbal interventions, especially for setting limits on student behavior, see Jones (1992).

- Jones, F. (1992). *Positive classroom discipline*. New York: McGraw-Hill.

Jonathan's Story

How noisy is too noisy for you? My tolerance for noise was higher than all the teachers I observed and assisted. But perhaps that was because I was too lenient with the students. The fact is that in some instances their behavior annoyed even me. So here's the technique my mentor suggested:

I quietly write the student's name on the board when he or she talks. The second time I write the student's name, he or she has detention with me. It sounded like a good idea so I tried it out.

I told the students what I was going to do, and they agreed that it was a reasonable thing to do. After that, everything worked out well. I had a wonderful time, everyone was quiet, and we had a productive lesson.

Jonathan adopted a management plan with a subtle but immediate signal. Like Thomas, Jonathan explained the plan to his students, including the consequences. Unlike Thomas, however, Jonathan's consequences were temperate and ones he himself took responsibility for enforcing. Most important, Jonathan provided his students the opportunity to understand and approve the plan. *Students are likely to abide by rules if they have had the opportunity to understand and agree to them.*

Reshaping Classroom Norms

Craig's Story

My last class can be fun to teach because they are lively. During my third week with them, however, I started to feel that the continuing conversations within the class were too disruptive and a challenge to my authority. Other students were beginning to call out "Be quiet." I began getting uptight and started yelling, singling out a few who were talking.

I'm not so sure this was the correct thing to do, but I do know that those who were singled out felt it was unfair because others were talking too. They gave me looks and comments that let me know they felt this way. Because my approach was confrontational, I felt I was destroying the rapport that I had been so proud of building. I also saw that the disorder had been making me so nervous that I overreacted.

Now, instead of a confrontational approach, I do what feels more comfortable. I stop the class until the students are quiet and then present the situation as a disruption to all of us, rather than as a challenge to my authority.

Rather than force them to comply with a system of rules and punishments, Craig treated his students as autonomous members of a learning community. He fostered their moral development, willingness to cooperate, and self-control by having them consider how their behavior was affecting others. That is, he used a "working with" rather than a "doing to" approach to instill norms of social responsibility. *A "working with" rather than a "doing to" approach promotes student maturity.*

Eliza's Story

My sixth-period class was the worst. No matter what I tried, I couldn't get them to stop talking. I tried assigning lunch detention, standing silent and looking stern, flashing the lights on and off, and finally one day, I tried yelling at them to be quiet. Nothing worked. At some point during each lesson, the noise would swell to an uproar. I could not understand why this class was so much more difficult than the others.

Yelling had been my last resort. Since that didn't work, I was baffled about what to do next. After brainstorming for a few days, I decided that I would treat them exactly as they had been treating me. Whenever one of the disruptive students would ask me a question or talk to me, I would interrupt or ignore him or her. I tried this for a couple of days with no reaction. On the third day, however, I got a reaction.

Kara raised her hand and asked, "Why are you being so mean to us?"

I replied that I was not trying to be mean, that I was just tired of the way I was being treated. I reviewed the single rule I had given them at the beginning of the year, that I would treat them with politeness and respect and that I expected the same in return. I told them that I had not been treated with politeness and respect and that their rudeness had rubbed off on me.

The silence was palpable. I stood there squarely so they could think about what I had just said. Then I asked them whether they liked the way I had been treating them for the past few days. Their answer was a unanimous no. Kara then apologized for the way she had been treating me, and I accepted her apology.

I then asked the class whether we could start from the beginning and treat each other with politeness and respect. Once again, their response was unanimous, this time a resounding yes. Since that day, I have had few if any problems with my sixth-period class.

Like Craig, Eliza had her students consider how their behavior affected others, her in particular. Not by enforcing a rule but by appealing to their sense of fairness, she elicited their commitment to treat her, and presumably the rest of the class, with politeness and respect. As a result, she, too, reshaped her class's norms into those of a socially responsible learning community, an approach requiring patience but offering the promise of lasting benefits.

Note to Craig's and Eliza's Stories: Creating a Caring Community

Rather than force compliance, Craig and Eliza each fostered their students' moral development by giving them the opportunity to make an informed ethical choice and then assume responsibility for their behavior. Such a student-directed management system contributes toward creating a caring community of learners.

- Kohn, A. (2006a). *Beyond discipline: From compliance to community, 10th anniversary edition*. Alexandria, VA: Association for Supervision and Curriculum Development.

These 10 novice teachers' stories present us with a continuum of effectiveness in managing the inevitable, a persistently noisy class. Their stories show us a progressive development from redefining themselves as a manager to assuming that power to effect an immediate strategy and finally to reshaping the class's norms. Where are you on this continuum?

8

When Your Normally Attentive Class Is Noisy

How can you engage (or reengage) your normally attentive but now noisy class? Of the six **novice teachers** in this chapter, the first four each advanced the lesson. The fifth became mired in discipline, and the sixth, doing neither, could only wonder how she could have regained her students' attention.

John's Story

The event took place while teaching an A.P. calculus class. The class consisted of 21 students, a combination of juniors and seniors. The students in this class are extremely grade conscious. This fact

(Continued)

(Continued)

works against my maintaining an effective classroom pace. The students know that a slower pace means less material on exams, which translates into higher grades for them.

On this day, the noise level in the class kept increasing. My request for silence had little effect. So I switched from a recitation format to a lecture format. Also, in an attempt to cover the intended material, I quickened my pace considerably. The noise level dropped, and the class attended to the lesson.

John's response to the increasing noise was subtle. He didn't moralize or lose his temper. Instead, he raised his students' level of anxiety by quickening the pace of the lesson. *Quickening the pace of a lesson is a useful technique but only when the potential for boredom is high, such as during a lecture or recitation, and the students are efficient learners who care about their grades.*

Referred to as "drill and kill," a **recitation** is a series of teacher questions each followed by a student's answer. This often monotonous but regrettably common teaching strategy is especially risky for novices, who have yet to master the art of asking an effective question, let alone of doing it spontaneously. Students quickly become bored with the interaction, which at any one time calls for the participation of only one student. Instead of a lecture, John could have engaged his students in a more creative learning experience as we'll see in the next **story.**

Notes to John's Story

Recitations

Some educators claim that a recitation is a useful instructional strategy because it offers students an opportunity to get feedback on their understanding of recent material and alerts them to the significant points. In addition, it enables teachers to assess their students' understandings.

- Farrar, M. (1986). Teacher questions: The complexity of the cognitively simple. *Instructional Science, 15*, 89–107.
- Gall, M. (1984). Synthesis of research on teachers' questioning. *Educational Leadership, 42*(3), 40–47.

Others claim that because the teacher controls the discourse, a recitation limits opportunities for authentic discussion and for students to frame their own questions.

- Dillon, J. T. (1988). *Questioning and teaching: A manual of practice*. New York: Teachers College Press.

Posing Effective Questions

Regardless of whether you use recitation as an instructional strategy, you still need to know how to pose an effective question. Groisser (1964) explains the characteristics of effective questions and how to use them to promote classroom discourse. For example, an effective question must be thought provoking. Thus, a "how," "why," or "what if" question is better than a "what" or "which" question. Besides, students are less likely to call out a response to a thought-provoking question because a clause or entire sentence rather than a single word or phrase is necessary.

The teacher needs to allow sufficient wait time for students to wrestle with such a question, perhaps even inviting them to jot down their ideas or consult with a neighbor before attempting a response. Mary Budd Rowe refers to this wait time as **wait time 1,** the length of the pause between the teacher's asking a question and calling on a student to answer. She defines **wait time 2** as the length of the pause between the student's answer and the teacher's response to that answer. Her claim is that increasing both wait times substantially improves students' comprehension and attitude.

- Groisser, P. (1964). *How to use the fine art of questioning*. Valley Stream, NY: Teachers Practical Press.
- Rowe, M. B. (1986). Wait time: Slowing down may be a way of speeding up! *Journal of Teacher Education, 37*(1), 43–50.

Liz's Story

My social studies class was starting a unit on economics, and I planned the first lesson with the idea that the students would need quite a bit of background information on the Supply and Demand Model before they could do any learning tasks themselves. I mistakenly believed that the students could handle a long lecture. Well, about halfway through my spiel, the noise became unbearable. I couldn't even hear my own voice. I started asking questions of particular students as a way to point out that they were not paying attention. The students looked discouraged, and their attitudes didn't improve at all with my questioning. So I decided to abandon the lecture, break them up into small groups, and give each group a topic I had planned to cover in my lecture. Luckily, I had supplies in the room that I could grab. Everyone in each group was assigned a production role, and each group was instructed to make a poster about its topic.

Doing this was actually frightening for me because I could imagine the students becoming noisier, even more out of control. I was pleasantly surprised when, after they received their supplies, the room became comparatively quiet. They got so involved in their research that they actually begged to stay longer so they could finish their posters.

I realized that just because I am standing at the front of the room, I am not necessarily in control and the students are not necessarily learning anything. I actually enjoy this spirited class very much. I have learned not to give them any slack when my lecture is brief, but now they know they can expect a rewarding experience afterwards, working to create their own understanding of the material.

In response to the mounting noise, both John and Liz changed their teaching strategy. Unlike John, Liz restructured her lesson entirely, involving her students in an active, creative learning experience, putting the responsibility for understanding the material squarely on their shoulders. In her desperation, she discovered that *a teacher can regain students' interest by involving them in an appealing learning activity.*

What's more, she realized that *rather than impose control, a teacher should foster students' self-control.* Last, she realized that telling isn't teaching. *Students can listen for only a short period of time. Then they need an opportunity to build their own understanding of the material.*

How could you spontaneously restructure one of your lessons?

Adrienne's Story

The event that sticks out in my mind occurred in my middle school on a Friday, the day after Rosh Hashanah. We had no classes on Rosh Hashanah, so when Friday arrived, school was the last place the students wanted to be. I could tell from the minute I walked into the building that it would be a hectic day. When classes began, my fears were confirmed. The students were rambunctious and had difficulty settling down. By second period, I was ready to pull my hair out.

Thankfully, I remembered a trick I learned at a school-sponsored seminar on **classroom management**. Some of the students were familiar with the management technique I used. I raised my hand and counted from 1 to 5 loudly enough to be heard. The students familiar with this technique caught on and began counting along. The others were confused as to what was going on and stopped their conversations. I was prepared to repeat this procedure as we were instructed, but fortunately this was not necessary. Once I had their attention, I explained the technique and continued to use it for the rest of the day with great success.

When I was introduced to this technique, I wasn't sure how well the students would respond. However, to my surprise and delight, it works beautifully, and my doubts about its effectiveness have disappeared.

Adrienne taught her students to respond to an obtrusive, brief, and immediately recognizable signal. What's more, the signal is nonverbal. *Nonverbal signals are better than verbal signals because they do not provoke defensive arguments or hostile confrontations.*

Tiffany's Story

I awoke that morning with a really bad cold, and over the course of the day, it developed into a case of laryngitis. By the afternoon, I could hardly talk at all and couldn't quiet the kids down to start the lesson. So I let my seventh graders know of my situation. At that point, I decided to give them some responsibility for managing the class. We were going to be doing some small-group activities, and I needed a way to get them back together as a whole class. So I let them suggest a signal they could all agree on so I wouldn't have to strain my voice. The signal would alert them to give me their attention.

After they made suggestions and I approved them, the kids voted on the signal they preferred. I then used that signal to get their attention for the rest of the period. The kids' participation in choosing the signal and the carefully planned lesson, one that kept them actively involved for the entire period, contributed toward the class's running smoothly.

By giving her students a share in choosing the signal, Tiffany fostered their commitment to it. Like Liz, she relaxed her own control to rely instead on their self-control, and she involved her students in an appealing learning activity.

Accordingly, rather than persisting with a lesson doomed to fail (and then blaming the failure on their students), all four teachers acted like a **classroom manager** rather than a **disciplinarian.** They controlled what they could, the execution of their lesson. *Teachers cannot control their students' behaviors, although they can influence and react to them. Teachers can, however, control their own behavior.*

Matt's Story

It started off with just a few of them chatting. I promptly made it clear that their talking was disruptive. I was trying to finish up the lesson so I did nothing more. Well, that was definitely a mistake. Now I had six people involved in conversations, which would stop when I told them to but then resume as soon as I did. I probably could have moved their seats, but with only a few minutes left, I didn't.

After two more warnings, I was at my wit's end. I told the entire class that because I had had to give them too many warnings, they were to remain in their seats when the bell rang, their next period being lunch. After the bell, I spent the next 40 seconds finishing my lesson. Then I took the next minute to explain why I had to keep them, why their actions were disruptive, and how their disruptions caused the entire class to have to stay. I got the class to acknowledge what had just happened, and at that point, I let them go to lunch, telling the select few troublemakers that they would not be sitting next to each other tomorrow.

Upon reflection, I realized I should not have punished the **good students** by keeping them all after the bell, and that my reprimanding the troublemakers did not have to be conducted in front of the entire class. So now I know that teachers should not punish everyone for the actions of a few, and those actions should be dealt with privately.

Matt learned one thing he should never do: *Never impose group punishment*. But he had yet to devise a strategy to deal with the class when it gets noisy, perhaps because he had yet to recognize his own contribution to the problem. *Only when you recognize your own contribution to a problem do you have any power to solve it*.

For example, he issued a set of warnings rather than explain his feelings. Instead of saying, "Your talking is disruptive," which is arguable, he should have told the class how he felt, saying something like this: "I am angry because the few minutes we have left are being wasted with side chatter." In other words, he needed to *address the situation, not the shortcomings of the student(s)*.

Second, he could have restructured the last few minutes of the lesson from a whole-class to an individual or paired activity. If he were giving some summarizing notes, he could instead have asked the students to make a list of summarizing points individually and then swap their list with a classmate. Then he might have advanced his lesson and avoided the mire of discipline.

Matt's response to their failure to heed his warnings was punishment. But *punishment does not deter* **misbehavior;** *it fosters resentment, not cooperation.* How could he have fostered their self-control instead?

Audrey's Story

As soon as I began the PowerPoint presentation, several students started talking. In order to advance the slides, I stood next to the SMART Board at the front of the room. When I stopped to pose a question, I instructed the students to take a minute to write down a response. Instead of following the directions, they simply started talking to one another. I tried calling the names of the students who were talking, but I got no response. The talking continued, and I began to feel helpless because I didn't know how to regain their attention.

How could Audrey have held her students' attention during her PowerPoint presentation? How could she have regained their attention?

9

When the Class Misuses Instructional Materials

Three **novice teachers** each planned an appealing activity for her students. The first teacher experienced utter chaos but made some effective changes for her later classes. The second averted chaos, but only barely. The third, who undertook the riskiest of activities, taking her students outside, succeeded without a problem. Why was she so successful?

Amy's Story

After finishing our units on the skeletal and digestive systems, my classes were ready to begin the lab that is the highlight of seventh-grade life science, the frog dissection. Because of our block rotation schedule, the fifth-period class was ahead of the others and would be the only class to do the dissection on this particular day, a Friday.

(Continued)

(Continued)

I told the students about the dissection and gave them the option to just watch if they felt uncomfortable morally, philosophically, or personally. But, of course, they all wanted to do it. Most would be working in groups of two, but some could dissect their own frog. For the **do-now,** the students were asked to write their feelings about doing the dissection, and everyone seemed excited to be doing it.

Chaos ruled for the entire period. I was frantically trying to go over the rules, pass out the dissecting tools, and warn the students of the hazards, especially in using the scalpel and probe. I read the steps of the lab aloud while demonstrating the technique on a frog. Some eager students, however, quickly began cutting up their frogs before I could tell them what they were looking at.

Other groups refused to touch their frogs and started shrieking, "Eeewww. It's alive!" or "Gross, it's breathing." So I went over to them and dissected their frogs myself. I tried to remain calm, but the situation was quickly getting so loud and out of control that I could barely contain my laughter.

Finally, when I gave the groups a few minutes to do their own exploring, they mutilated the frogs, sadistically cutting out their eyeballs and stabbing them with their probes. At the end of the period, I had the students throw away their frogs and clean out their dissecting pans. What they didn't do, however, was clean the surface of their tables. So when the next class came in, those students got all charged up about the frog parts (e.g., eggs, skin, and eyeballs) littering their tabletops.

Upon reflection, I realized this experience was of little or no value to this class. So for my classes on Monday, I turned the lab into a 2-day activity where I could take one period just to explain the rules and demonstrate the procedure. I also took more time to explain the moral issues and why they needed to behave maturely. When the time came for these classes to dissect their frogs, **classroom management** was no longer a problem, and the students really learned from the experience.

Amy was successful on Monday because she took the time to communicate with her students. She stressed the moral issues in doing the dissection and used those issues to justify her expectation that they behave maturely. *Students* *need to understand the rationale behind a rule, **routine,** or expectation, that each is not simply an arbitrary attempt to control their behavior.*

Second, by extending the activity to a 2-day experience, Amy disconnected her doing the demonstration from their doing the dissection. During her presentation, the students were no longer sitting in pairs, and, more important, they did not have the materials in hand. *Materials should be distributed no sooner than immediately before each student or group is to use them, and they should be collected no later than immediately after each student or group is finished with them.* Deferring the distribution of materials would have precluded her Friday students from dissecting their frog before she had instructed them fully. Likewise, advancing the collection of materials would preclude students from toying with them after completing an activity.

Amy used a routine, the do-now, to ensure an orderly beginning to her lesson. *If used consistently, a routine minimizes the time and energy needed to direct a regular classroom event.* For the do-now, instead of asking her students to write down their feelings about doing the dissection, Amy could have asked each of them, given the hazards, to propose a list of safety rules. *Students are likely to abide by a rule they had a share in creating.*

To ensure an orderly ending to her lesson, Amy needed a routine for cleaning up. *Cleaning up should never be left for the very end of a class.* Plan instead to close each lesson with a redundant activity after the cleanup, such as a second summarizing activity. Then the cleanup need not be rushed. All materials can be cleaned, collected, inspected, counted, and either put away or rearranged for the next class.

Plan as well to assign cleanup roles (e.g., desk wiper) so as to delegate responsibility, concentrate accountability, and reduce traffic congestion in the classroom. *Students,* however, *need opportunities to learn and practice a routine,* including the duties associated with each role.

Amy also needed to stop the students who were shrieking as soon as they started to overreact. Instead of doing the dissection for them, she should have given them an opportunity to calm down. She could have taken their materials and given them a piece of text, such as one on frog anatomy, and a definite assignment, and then invited them to signal her if and when they were ready to begin the dissection again.

Last, Amy needed to give her students a task to complete along with the dissection, one requiring them to produce evidence of having reflected thoughtfully during the activity. *Hands-on is not enough; the task also has to be brains-on.*

For example, she could have assigned each student to choose one structure in the frog's anatomy and write three to five sentences to explain how its design is suited to the frog's way of life. *Students need to produce some evidence of cognitive work during an activity.*

Then, instead of giving them unstructured time for exploration, which they squandered mutilating their frog, Amy could have directed them to study its entire anatomy purposefully. *Unstructured time generates boredom, restlessness, and disruption.*

None of Amy's students were morally opposed to doing the dissection. Some, however, could have been. How would you have responded to a student's moral opposition?

Mandy's Story

My clothing construction students were about to pin their pattern to their fabric and transfer the construction marks. The students were working in pairs. I distributed to each pair a bin with pins, a pin cushion, shears, tracing paper, and a tracing wheel, and I handed each pair a yardstick. Once they got their materials, I explained how to use them. The first class went fairly well, except for the fact that I spoke too quickly, so the students missed some of the directions. Because of this, I ended up answering a lot of extra questions. That was the first lesson I learned that day, to speak slowly. Otherwise, the pairs completed the activity successfully and enjoyed doing it.

Then came the second class. Once again, I distributed the materials to minimize student traffic. But this time, "weapons" and "athletic gear" emerged. Before I knew it, a couple of "sword fights" were on one side of the room and some "hockey games" on the other. Right then I knew this activity was going to be a disaster.

I had to get their attention quickly so I let out an ear-piercing whistle. Everyone stopped immediately. Next, I told them that those who could not use the equipment properly would have to complete the activity during lunch. That was the second lesson I learned that day, that they all want to have lunch with their friends. By the time I was ready to wrap up the lesson, all the pairs had finished the activity successfully.

Unlike Amy, Mandy averted chaos by immediately stopping the class with a brief but intrusive signal. Better yet, the signal was nonverbal. *Nonverbal signals are better than verbal signals because they do not provoke defensive arguments or hostile confrontations.* Then a warning to those who would misuse the materials gave her students the opportunity to control their own behavior. *Rather than impose control, a teacher should foster students' self-control.* Aside from the temperate but disagreeable consequence, her warning worked because her students wanted to participate in the activity. *A teacher can regain students' interest by involving them in an appealing learning activity.*

Mandy had an efficient routine for distributing (and collecting) materials. She used bins, which are especially useful when the items are numerous or small. However, like Amy, Mandy handed out the materials too soon, before she'd had a chance to explain their use. Sometimes a teacher needs to distribute a piece of equipment to instruct students in its use. *If students must hold a piece of equipment so you can instruct them in its use, then distribute just that piece of equipment.*

Mandy tells us that during her first class, because she spoke too quickly, students missed part of her directions. Novice teachers, because their anxiety drives them to rush, need to make a deliberate effort to slow down. Still, students are likely to miss directions for other reasons as well, such as being distracted or coming to class late. Therefore, *students need a set of written directions.* (In Chapter 4, read about the chaos Melissa, Charlotte, and Tara each experienced when their students did not have a simple set of written directions.)

Why was Mandy's warning likely to be more effective than Tara's (Chapter 4)?

Note to Mandy's Story:
Logical Consequence or Punishment

Mandy offered her students a choice, either comply or face the **logical consequence,** namely, having to complete the lab during their lunch period. A logical consequence is defined as a reasonable outcome the teacher imposes that is directly related to the **misbehavior.** Dreikurs and Grey (1968) and Levin and Nolan (2007) advocate imposing a logical consequence as long as the student sees the relationship between the misbehavior and the consequence. Then the teacher is not cast in the role of punisher, and the consequence, unlike a punishment, would imply no anger or moral judgment.

- Dreikurs, R., & Grey, L. (1968). *A new approach to discipline: Logical consequences.* New York: Hawthorne.
- Levin, J., & Nolan, J. F. (2007). *Principles of classroom management: A professional decision-making model* (5th ed.). Boston: Allyn & Bacon.

Kohn (2006a), however, argues that the term "logical consequence" is simply a euphemism for punishment, that students are not likely to see the connection between the misbehavior and the consequence, that they are still likely to see the teacher as the punisher, and that the act of imposing a consequence is, like all punishment, coercive rather than instructive.

- Kohn, A. (2006a). *Beyond discipline: From compliance to community, 10th anniversary edition.* Alexandria, VA: Association for Supervision and Curriculum Development.

Ariel's Story

The first activity I planned for the ecology unit was a lab to study an ecosystem. In this lab, the students had to use a meter stick to measure 1 square meter of an ecosystem and then list all the populations they observed there. Before the lab, I introduced them to some concepts and the idea that organisms interact with each other and their environment.

The day before this lab, I had mixed feelings about taking this class of 27 students outside. What am I thinking of? But the next day, everything went as planned. The materials were ready for the students to use and the area was suitable for the activity. The students also understood that if they didn't behave appropriately, they would have no other opportunities to work outside. Overall, I was pleased with the work they did and would be willing to take them out again.

How did Ariel promote the success of her lesson? Why was her lesson more successful than either Amy's or Mandy's? Why was the timing of Ariel's warning more effective than the timing of either Mandy's or, in Chapter 4, Tara's?

When Students Don't Do Their Homework

Getting students to do and hand in their homework involves **routines** for both the teacher and the students. In the first **story,** David learns that he has to follow the established routine to communicate the assignment to his students. In the second story, Betsy establishes a routine for holding her students accountable for doing their homework.

David's Story

I started teaching in the middle of an academic year, when the permanent teacher took a maternity leave. Before she left, she explained to me her routines for assigning homework and starting each lesson. She wrote the homework assignment and **do-now** for the day on the board and trained the students, as soon as they came in, to copy the assignment and then start the do-now.

> For my first day, I taught a lesson about irregular verbs. I made sure I had the do-now on the board, but I didn't write down the homework assignment. As soon as the students came in, they began working on the do-now. The lesson was a success. With 1 minute remaining, I handed out a worksheet for homework and told them it would be due tomorrow. I went home feeling good about my first day.
>
> The next day, I asked the students to hand in their homework. They responded by saying, "What homework?" I got angry and yelled at them for not having done the homework. They told me that it wasn't written on the board so they didn't think it was homework. I ended up reassigning it, but I made sure this time that I wrote it on the board. My students handed in the worksheet the following day.

David realized that he needed to follow the previous teacher's routine for communicating the homework assignment. *If used consistently, a routine minimizes the time and energy needed to direct a regular classroom event.* If he wanted to change the routine, he would have to direct his students explicitly and then provide them with feedback and reminders.

Just as David needed a routine for communicating the assignment, teachers also need a routine for collecting, reviewing, evaluating, and returning the assignment promptly, as well as for recording the grades and otherwise holding their students accountable for doing it. Inasmuch as many secondary school teachers see more than 100 students per day, the commitment to process homework daily may be too onerous for a **novice teacher,** whose time might be better spent developing lessons. Therefore, if you do assign daily homework, consider a routine in which you walk around during the do-now crediting each student who has completed the homework. Likewise, consider collecting and reviewing only a sample of students' work each day or all the students' work but only once per week.

Note to David's Story: Routines

Teachers structure their learning environment with routines to manage both student work and regular classroom events, such as beginning and ending each lesson, distributing and collecting materials, and using classroom space.

- Evertson, C. (1987). Managing classrooms: A framework for teachers. In D. Berliner & B. Rosenshine (Eds.), *Talks to teachers* (pp. 54–75). New York: Random House.

Betsy's Story

The biggest problem I had with my students was getting them to turn in their homework. Although I kept telling them it was important to complete their assignments, I was still receiving only a handful of papers from each class. So my problem was how to get them to take their homework seriously.

I decided to adopt a strategy a colleague of mine used. He made his students accountable by having them explain in a letter why they didn't do their homework. From there, he would decide whether he would excuse them, give them an extension to complete the assignment, or speak to their parent or guidance counselor.

Thinking about something similar for my own classroom, I came up with a Homework Contract that would require the students to write down why they didn't do the assignment and then sign the document. The first day, many of my students were displeased with this new procedure. They didn't like the idea that they would be accountable for their missing assignments. The day after the Homework Contract went into effect, however, almost all my students completed and handed in their homework. Since I instituted the routine, I've received most of the homework most of the time.

Here is the form each student must sign:

WARNING

You have not done your homework, but you are still being held accountable!

You will not be permitted to leave this classroom without completing this form. Remember, homework is crucial to your success in this class.

Too many missing homework assignments will result in a phone call or letter home and a notice to your guidance counselor.

In the space below, please write out your reason for not completing the assignment.

_____

_____

_____

_____

_____

_____

_____

_____

_____

Title of the assignment _____

_____

Signature _____

Date _____

Betsy established a routine to demonstrate that she is serious about homework. She devised a document in which she reiterates her expectations, the rationale, and the consequences and then requires her students to justify in writing their lapse. In the process, she accumulates a file to temper the complaints of a grade-conscious student or parent.

Betsy gets most of her students to do most of the assignments. However, no teacher can expect all the students to do a particular assignment. Therefore, *do not make the success of your lesson dependent on all your students having done their homework.* For example, if you ask them to prepare a chart or bring an item from home, make sure you have spares so you can expect them to participate even if they didn't do the homework.

How do your values and beliefs about homework compare with those implied in Betsy's Homework Contract?

Note to Betsy's Story: Homework

Notwithstanding the controversy over the usefulness of homework, Good and Brophy (2008) recommend that teachers make clear the purpose and importance of an assignment along with their expectations. Then, if a student who can do the homework fails either to complete or submit it, the teacher should require him or her to do so during a free period or after school.

- Good, T. L., & Brophy, J. E. (2008). *Looking in classrooms* (10th ed.). Boston: Pearson.

Kohn (2006a), on the other hand, might object to Betsy's Homework Contract as coercive, recommending instead that she ask the students themselves, either as individuals or as a class, to devise a plan for submitting their assignments regularly. More fundamentally, he would question whether the assignment was worth doing and whether the students had any freedom to choose the task.

- Kohn, A. (2006a). *Beyond discipline: From compliance to community, 10th anniversary edition*. Alexandria, VA: Association for Supervision and Curriculum Development.

Most fundamentally, Kohn (2006b) would question whether homework promotes learning.

- Kohn, A. (2006b). *The homework myth: Why our kids get too much of a bad thing*. Cambridge, MA: Da Capo Press.

When There's a
Threat to Student
Safety

Teachers are responsible for providing a standard of care commensurate with their students' maturity and the hazards of the activity. Generally, initial management interventions should be subtle, but when student safety is at risk, the intervention must be as intrusive and direct as necessary to neutralize the threat immediately.

A threat to student safety can be physical, social, or psychological. The first two **stories** are about providing a **physically safe learning environment,** one in which the teacher models and the students practice techniques to protect themselves, each other, and the environment from physical harm. The third story is about providing a **socially and psychologically safe learning environment.** In such an environment, students interact respectfully and supportively, each feeling valued and capable of both learning and contributing to the learning of others.

Stephanie's Story

The students in my seventh-period food preparation class were grilling and carving meats. Because of the relatively high hazard level, I needed to ensure that they were working safely. When I tried to quiet them down for cleanup directions, however, I got no response. I tried again, asking politely, but again, no response.

At his point, I was furious and yelled, "Kids! Be quiet!" Finally, I was able to give them the cleanup directions, and after they cleaned up, they returned to their seats. I sat at the desk and said nothing. Feeling disappointed, I continued to sit there staring and motionless, flooded with frustration and confusion.

Next I talked to them on a personal level. I talked to them about respect, safety, learning, and acceptable behavior. I felt relieved, and from their expressions, I knew they understood. Ever since that talk, the class has been more respectful and responsive.

Before having her students begin the activity, Stephanie needed to have established safety rules and **routines,** including a cleanup routine and a signal for their immediate attention in case of an emergency. *If used consistently, a routine minimizes the time and energy needed to direct a regular classroom event. Students,* however, *need opportunities to learn and practice a routine.* Stephanie should therefore expect to have to provide them with reminders and feedback.

Fortunately, Stephanie had not left the cleanup for the very end of class. To ensure that it is thorough and orderly, *cleaning up should never be left for the very end of a class.* As a result, Stephanie had the opportunity after the cleanup to speak to her students calmly about her expectations and the rationale for them. *Students need to understand the rationale behind a rule, routine, or expectation, that each is not simply an arbitrary attempt to control their behavior.*

Cynthia's Story

On this Friday morning, I was to perform a demonstration using liquid nitrogen. I had 12 new students in my class of 27. The new students had come into the class 4 weeks into the school year, after we had already completed half the chapter. The liquid nitrogen demonstration was dangerous enough to perform without adding the uncertainty of new students, but I had promised I would do it that day and had explained to the students the safety precautions. Besides, it was a perfect demonstration for introducing the properties of matter.

The class was spellbound. One student, John, asked if he could touch the beaker that contained the liquid nitrogen. I, of course, said "No," adding that the beaker was so cold that if he touched it, his fingers would freeze. I also showed him and emphasized to the class the protective wear I had on. After seeing a flower shatter into pieces after being lowered into the liquid nitrogen and then smacked on the tabletop, the students began to understand the danger and obeyed the safety rules.

After the lesson was over, the bell rang, and most of the students moved past the demonstration table staying a safe distance from the liquid nitrogen. John, however, tried to come close to the table. Thinking of his safety, I blocked him by standing between him and the table as I escorted him to the door and chatted with him about how neat the experiment was.

Cynthia had explained the safety precautions in advance. Even so, she was alert to a challenge and responded by redirecting John's attention while thwarting his approach. Her intervention was swift but discreet, no more intrusive than necessary to neutralize the threat. Although she chatted with him about the experiment, her blocking him and escorting him to the door were nonverbal responses to his challenge. *Nonverbal interventions are better than verbal interventions because they do not provoke defensive arguments or hostile confrontations.*

Natalie's Story

As a physical education and health teacher, I am teaching my students about human reproduction. I knew this was going to be a challenging topic because of my students' misconceptions and the improper terms they use for the parts of the male and female reproductive systems.

(Continued)

(Continued)

The students are already dealing with issues of pregnancy and sexually transmitted diseases, so I wanted them to take this lesson seriously.

Prior to beginning the lesson, I expressed my concern and hope that we could get through the lesson without inappropriate language and jokes. I also told them that they were welcome to ask any question as long as it is phrased in a manner appropriate to the classroom. If they had trouble phrasing the question, they could ask me privately, and I would phrase it appropriately for them.

My students agreed and have been trying hard to be mature in dealing with human reproduction. By expressing my concern and explaining my boundary beforehand and having them agree to my terms, I kept the discussion mature while letting them know that they can still ask me any question and get an answer.

Natalie's challenge was to create a socially and psychologically safe environment for her students to study human reproduction. Unlike Stephanie, but like Cynthia, she foresaw the threat. Accordingly, in advance of her lesson, she planned the rules and routine for appropriate communication, discussed and justified them with her students, and gave them the opportunity to understand and agree to them. *Students are likely to abide by rules if they have had the opportunity to understand and agree to them.*

Natalie does not explain how she helped her students construct an appropriately worded question privately without interrupting her lesson and introducing **dead time.** One approach Natalie could have used was to give each of her students a few index cards at the outset and invite them, as the lesson progressed, to write down their emerging questions. She could then collect, shuffle, and rephrase the questions as necessary. The advantages of such an approach would be not only to avoid dead time but to enable her students to ask their questions anonymously.

Stephanie, Cynthia, and Natalie each calmly explained and justified their expectations to their students. Second, they each involved and expected to continue involving their students in appealing activities, such as using novel materials or relating a concept to everyday life. *Activities in which students can work together, choose their task, be creative, use novel materials, imagine a novel situation, or relate a concept to everyday life appeal to students.* Because of their approaches to teaching their particular subject matter, their students willingly cooperated with their rules and routines.

How do you provide for your students' physical, social, and psychological safety?

Note: Safety

Safety is a basic human need (Maslow, 1968). Accordingly, to take the risks necessary to learn, students must feel physically, socially, and psychologically safe in the classroom.

- Maslow, A. (1968). *Toward a psychology of being.* New York: Van Nostrand

When There's
a Mishap

Two **novice teachers** each maintained their composure and resisted the tendency to be diverted from their lesson when a mishap occurred in their classrooms. Sally and Len each continued to be the model of a rational, temperate, consistent, and positive adult even under pressure.

Sally's Story

I imagine most novice teachers experience an embarrassing moment. I am no exception. I was writing notes on a transparency and projecting them for my seventh-period language arts class when the purple marker I was using exploded in my hand and leaked ink all over me, my clothes, the desk, and the floor.

These students are the first ones to laugh at someone else's mistake or misfortune. So when the marker exploded, I just threw it away, grabbed another, and continued my lesson as if nothing had happened.

Continuing without explanation, Sally resisted the tendency to be diverted from her lesson. Fortunately, she had an extra marker. Like Sally, *have handy, for both you and your students, extra supplies and equipment,* such as markers, chalk, transparencies, paper towels, books, projector bulbs, and extension cords. And, like Sally, guard your instructional time. *For every minute you divert your students from the course of your lesson, you will lose several times that amount trying to reengage them.*

Len's Story

Murphy said, "If something can go wrong, it will!" And that's what happened to me the day I planned to demonstrate Charles's Law for my physical science class. Not only wouldn't the hot plate heat fast enough, but nothing else went well either. When these kinds of things happen, I ask myself, "What can I learn from these mishaps?" In this case, I learned the importance of having a backup plan. I resorted to asking the class questions about what should have happened and why.

I was careful to explain to the class that I had made a mistake in not having tested the hot plate or having another one handy. "Teachers are human and make mistakes, too," I said. The next day, I repeated an abridged version of the demonstration and went on from there. I know the students appreciated my honesty.

Like Sally, Len conserved his instructional time, substituting a set of "what if" and "why" questions for the aborted demonstration. *Punctuating a lecture with thought-provoking questions (typically "why," "how," or "what if" questions) can stimulate interest.* However, improvising a few thought-provoking questions is a risky strategy for novice teachers, who have yet to master the art of asking an effective question, let alone of doing it spontaneously. Consequently, the strategy can degenerate into a **recitation.** To promote a more extensive and thoughtful consideration of his questions, among even timid students, Len could have had his students formulate and justify a written prediction in pairs, with several pairs then reporting to the rest of the class.

Second, Len recognized his failure to test the hot plate or have another one handy. *Only when you recognize your own contribution to a problem do you have any power to solve it.* He also admitted his mistake to his students. *Don't be afraid to admit your mistakes.* Teachers are not perfect. (No one could stand a teacher who was.) Rather than being perfect, *honest communication is fundamental to your relationships with your students.*

Last, as they each continued their lesson, Sally and Len maintained their composure. Regardless of the unexpected, teachers need to be the model of a rational, temperate, consistent, and positive adult, the only such model some of their students may ever see.

Note: Moral Authority

In maintaining their composure, Sally and Len each continued to be the model of a rational, temperate, consistent, and positive adult. According to Ginott (1972), they each maintained their position as the moral authority by demonstrating self-control even under pressure.

- Ginott, H. G. (1972). *Teacher and child: A book for parents and teachers.* New York: Macmillan.

When a Tragic
Event Affects the
School Community

One **novice teacher** earned her students' respect by listening to and accepting their expressions of grief. Although the particular tragedy affecting Bridget's school community is rare, other tragic events, such as the loss from a natural disaster, fire, accident, illness, criminal act, or war, are all too common.

Bridget's Story

When I arrived at school on Monday morning, the student parking lot was empty, and the flag was at half-mast. Mr. Cedric, the English teacher, had died over the weekend. The principal held a teachers' meeting and told us that the start of school would be delayed an hour, we should keep things as normal as possible, but grieving students would have places to go throughout the day.

(Continued)

(Continued)

When the students arrived, many were hugging each other and crying in the halls. The bell to signal the beginning of homeroom rang, and the halls were eerily silent. I entered my homeroom. Nobody spoke. When the announcements came on, the principal delivered the sad news. Some students went out into the hall to cry. The rest of them, many teary-eyed, stayed in their seats. I read to the students a list of places they could go if they were feeling too upset to remain in class.

During the first period, I tried to begin the lesson, but I couldn't. The Roman Empire seemed so irrelevant in this context. Some of my students were crying, and others had a blank look on their face. I asked whether they would like to take the first 10 minutes to talk with each other or just to sit and think. They seemed grateful for this suggestion. A few of the girls who were crying gathered in the back of the room. I had graded their tests over the weekend but decided not to return them right away. I figured receiving their grades might create additional stress for some of them.

After the first 10 minutes, I announced I would begin the lesson. I told the students they could excuse themselves at any time if they were feeling overwhelmed and wanted to visit one of the grief sites. Three girls who were crying left the room. The rest of the class quietly followed along as I drew on a transparency a time line of the emperors and projected it onto the screen. I had also planned some group work for them, but somehow I didn't think they'd be up to it. I think just sitting and listening to me was all they could do. Some looked relieved just to have something else to think about.

My other classes were scheduled for a test that day. Many of the girls in these classes are on the basketball team, and Mr. Cedric's wife is their coach. These girls were very upset. Some of them left class, but most stayed in the classroom. I passed out the test and told them that today they need not write anything more than their name, that they could take the test home and return it on Wednesday. At the end of the class, one student thanked me for the extension on the test and said that I was nice to do that.

Mr. Cedric was a young teacher. His death at age 28 was a shock and loss to the community. I am still an outsider here. I could express my sympathy but did not feel the loss the way many of my students and fellow teachers did.

The students saw that I was sympathetic. I treated them with respect and kindness. I think just listening and being sympathetic is all a teacher can do in a situation like this. One thing I've learned is that young people can sense your emotions and good intentions. They knew that I was concerned about them. I put their feelings first, and they responded well to that.

A teacher should be strict about students' behavior but permissive about their feelings. Although as an outsider Bridget could not empathize with her students' sense of loss, she accepted their expressions of grief. First, she was flexible about conducting her lessons, knowing that under such a circumstance, her delaying the start of the lesson or postponing the test would hardly set a precedent. Second, she extended to her students the precious gift of listening.

Last, she followed her principal's directions, permitting her students to visit a grief site rather than trying to be the counselor herself. A teacher's role is complicated enough without trying to be a counselor, psychologist, or social worker. *Teachers need to recognize and accept their limitations.*

Note: Students' Feelings

Ginott (1972) explains that a teacher should allow students to express how they feel because, unlike behavior, people cannot control how they feel. Accordingly, he warns against a teacher's belittling students' feelings or otherwise responding in such a way as to cause them discomfort, guilt, embarrassment, or shame. Instead, he explains the importance of listening to students and responding authentically to them because "nothing defeats him [a teacher] more than phoniness" (p. 121).

- Ginott, H. G. (1972). *Teacher and child: A book for parents and teachers.* New York: Macmillan.

PART II
Discipline Problems

When a Good Student Violates a Minor Rule

Two **novice teachers** each found an alternative to punishment when a **good student** violated a minor rule. The term "good student" refers here to a student who understands and accepts classroom rules as reasonable, whose infractions are occasional at most and are the result of forgetfulness or lapses in self-control rather than defiance.

Breeanne's Story

One day, my middle school students were doing presentations in front of the class. During one presentation, the principal slipped into the classroom and made herself comfortable in the back row.

As the presentation continued, the unthinkable happened. A student's cell phone beeped. As I turned in the direction of the beep, I knew exactly whose phone it was. Only one face had the look of utter terror, Bardo's. I am still not sure who was more mortified, Bardo or I. Not wanting to distract further from the presentation, I tiptoed over to him to wait for an appropriate moment to address the situation.

Bardo, like most of the others, tries so hard to be good, but we all make mistakes. I like to give this kind of kid a second chance, but with the principal standing right there, I wasn't sure whether she expected me to confiscate his phone. Moments later, she got up to leave and on the way out, whispered to him, "Keep that cell phone off, huh?"

After she left, Bardo and I both heaved a sigh of relief. Leaning over, I told him how lucky he was that she made light of the situation. He just smiled. He had already realized the extent of his luck and thanked me for my understanding. I believe that in this kind of situation, showing compassion is more important than making a scene over a minor offense.

Bardo understood and accepted the rule. He probably had just forgotten to turn off his phone. The beep alone was sufficient notice that he had violated the rule and disrupted the presentation, and with Breeanne's look, that he was caught red-handed and could be punished. But Breeanne approached him with compassion, not anger, with a "working with" rather than a "doing to" attitude. *A "working with" rather than a "doing to" approach promotes student maturity.*

Bardo saw that Breeanne was on his side. *Teachers are more likely to be successful with students who see the teacher as on their side.* Fortunately for both, the principal was also on his side. She too understood that *good discipline is achieved only through repeated kindnesses.*

How should Breeanne have responded if Bardo's cell phone had been a recurring distraction? If he understood and accepted the rule that the cell phone needs to be turned off during class, then the issue would still be his forgetfulness rather than his defiance. But given its recurrence, he would need to take responsibility for the problem explicitly; that is, he would need to formulate a plan to prevent the beeps once and for all and to make a commitment to abide by that plan. Only if he failed to take responsibility would Breeanne have to offer him a choice with express consequences in accordance with the school policy.

Note to Breeanne's Story: Minor Misbehavior

A teacher needs to weigh the cost of intervening against the cost of the **misbehavior**. Minor rule violations are often better ignored, at least temporarily, so as not to disrupt an ongoing lesson. *Ignore behaviors that hardly interfere with teaching or learning.* A teacher needs to attend immediately to minor rule violations, however, when the misbehavior occurs repeatedly, intensifies, or seems about to spread.

- Good, T. L., & Brophy, J. E. (2008). *Looking in classrooms* (10th ed.). Boston: Pearson.

Todd's Story

During the last few minutes of class, I do not allow my students to get out of their seats. When they remain seated, they are more manageable than when they wander about. I also have a problem with students sitting on their desk. So occasionally I also have to ask them to sit in their chair.

One day, near the end of class, I noticed that Aaron was sitting on his desk. Instead of telling him what to do, I used my hands to frame my view of him and asked, "What's wrong with this picture?" Turning to me, he replied, "I shouldn't be sitting on my desk." He then sat in his chair.

I was pleased because I knew that he understood what I expected and responded without my having to tell him. I like it when a little reminder goes a long way.

Todd needed to give Aaron only a hint to obey the rule. The hint proved to be sufficient because Aaron understood and accepted the rule and was willing to cooperate.

Thus Todd, instead of having to issue a direct order, which is more likely to engender defiance than cooperation, could simply prompt Aaron to exercise his self-control. *Rather than impose control, a teacher should foster students' self-control.* Todd was also effective because when he corrected Aaron, he didn't criticize him, make an example of him, or preach to him. He addressed only the situation. Teachers should *address the situation, not the shortcomings of the student(s).*

What if Aaron had not cooperated in response to Todd's hint? Then Todd would have had to progress to a more intrusive intervention. Todd could have approached Aaron discreetly and told him what he needed to do and why, saying, for example, "I need you to sit in your chair so we can have an orderly close to the lesson." *Students need to understand the rationale behind a rule, **routine,** or expectation, that each is not simply an arbitrary attempt to control their behavior.*

If Aaron continued to refuse to sit in his chair, Todd could then press further for his cooperation by explaining how his behavior was affecting others. For example, Todd could say, "Your not sitting in your chair will postpone the lesson closure for everybody." Only if necessary would Todd progress to the next step, offering Aaron a choice with consequences: "Aaron, you have a choice. You can sit in your chair now, or you and I can discuss your behavior later."

Todd could calmly and routinely manage this series of progressively more direct and intrusive interventions only if he had already devised a systematic management plan. *Teachers need a systematic management plan ranging from subtle to progressively more direct and intrusive interventions.*

Todd and Breeanne could each protect their learning environment with a minimally intrusive strategy by attributing their students' infractions to forgetfulness or lapses in self-control rather than to defiance. *Resist the impulse to attribute minor infractions to defiance.* Accordingly, they could continue their lesson without having to issue either an order or a punishment. *Issuing an order promotes defiance, not cooperation.* And *punishment does not deter misbehavior; it fosters resentment, not cooperation.*

Note to Todd's Story: Systematic Management Plan

Teachers need a systematic management plan to respond calmly and consistently to ordinary classroom misbehaviors. Levin and Nolan (2007) advocate a model that features a hierarchy of responses ranging from subtle interventions, in which the student has an opportunity to exercise self-control, to progressively more intrusive and teacher-directed interventions. How does your hierarchy of interventions compare with the one proposed for Todd?

- Levin, J., & Nolan, J. F. (2007). *Principles of classroom management: A professional decision-making model* (5th ed.). Boston: Allyn & Bacon.

Canter and Canter (2001) recommend specific strategies for direct and intrusive interventions.

- Canter, L., & Canter, M. (2001). *Assertive discipline: Positive behavior management for today's classrooms* (Rev. ed.). Los Angeles: Canter Associates.

When You Have
a Class Clown

A class clown is a student, usually male, who, through his antics, seeks to dominate class interactions in order to gain his classmates' attention. The following **stories** each feature one of two strategies to mitigate the class clown's disruptions. In the first two stories, Danny and Eric each dare the class clown to take center stage. In the last two, Ellen and Millie each push him off the stage.

DARING THE CLASS
CLOWN TO TAKE CENTER STAGE

Danny's Story

Five minutes into class, I was able to pick out the class clown. He made sure all the attention was on him. On any other day, I might not have minded so much, but this was my very first day. I knew that if I let him continue, I would never be able to control the class. I first asked him to settle down. This worked for about 30 seconds. Then he not only continued to tease some of the kids but started distracting me as well.

(Continued)

(Continued)

At this point, I was doing a demonstration for which I needed an assistant. Who better to choose? I asked for a volunteer while one of his arms happened to be raised. Having little choice, he came up to help me. Although he now had the entire class staring at him, this was not the kind of attention he wanted.

Since then, he has calmed down. I wouldn't call him my best student, but I can see that by stopping him that first day, I passed his test. He knows I won't tolerate his attempts to dominate the class.

Danny communicated an implicit warning: "I am the authority here. If you want attention, you just might get it, but on my terms, not yours."

Eric's Story

The kids had just come from gym for their last class on an unseasonably warm Friday afternoon. They were bouncing off the walls, bursting with energy and planning their weekend. I had to take several minutes just to get them in their seats and ready to work. Classroom **routines** were a distant memory. These kids wanted nothing to do with learning. My desperate attempts to capture their attention were exactly that, desperate. After several minutes of coaxing, however, I got to start my lesson.

The next 30 minutes were touch and go. The kids were poorly behaved, but we came close to completing the lesson. During the last few minutes, however, the most dominant kid, the perennial class clown, was vying with me for control. After all this, was he going to prevent me from closing the lesson?

Rather than waste my time with warnings or threats, I enlisted his help. First, I tried having him assist me from his seat, but that didn't work because with all the noise, the others couldn't hear him. So, again in desperation, I brought him up to join me at the front of the room. It worked wonderfully. The other kids listened and laughed as he summarized the lesson. Of course, I had to correct his blunders, but everyone in the class thoroughly enjoyed his humorous but informative closure to the lesson.

Both Danny and Eric acted like a **classroom manager** rather than a **disciplinarian.** That is, they concentrated on continuing the lesson rather than on treating the **misbehavior.** They each took a risk, daring their class clown to take center stage, but ended up creating a novel situation that captured the attention of the other students and redirected the behavior of the clown. *Give a class clown attention but for only appropriate behavior.*

PUSHING THE CLASS CLOWN OFF THE STAGE

Ellen's Story

I especially remember Tim. He was an intelligent boy but also the class clown, always talking and interrupting the lesson with his jokes. Finishing his own work quickly, he would then disturb his classmates and disrupt the entire class. At first, I tried directing specific questions toward him, but this strategy didn't work. He was on center stage. In spite of being disruptive, however, I must say he did his assignments, even correcting them for extra credit, and otherwise showed concern for his grades.

One day during class, I changed his seat. He certainly didn't like that, but the immediate result was that he was more attentive. When the class was over, I explained to him the reason for the change, that he needed to pay more attention and show more respect to his classmates and me. Finally, I told him that because he was an intelligent boy, I had high expectations for him.

During the days that followed, his behavior improved. Yes, he has his ups and downs, but all in all, he is more attentive and respectful.

Ellen was effective, first, not so much because she changed his seat but because she explained to him privately why she had done so. *A private conversation preserves the student's or students' dignity, thereby forestalling a defensive or hostile response.* Second, in her explanation, she affirmed her high expectations for him. *Communicating high expectations is likely to improve student behavior as well as achievement.* And last, in the context of her high expectations and his concern for his grades, he could understand why the seat change was for his benefit. *Students need to understand the rationale behind a rule, routine, or expectation, that each is not simply an arbitrary attempt to control their behavior.*

Nevertheless, class clowns are persistent. Danny and Eric were effective enough to complete their lesson, but for a lasting solution, a teacher would need to persevere over weeks and even months to help a student improve his self-control. Specifically, first a teacher would need to speak with him in private to make sure he was aware of the behavior and why it cannot be tolerated and then get him to take responsibility for the behavior and make a commitment to change. *If students have made a commitment to a rule, especially one they had a share in creating, they are likely to correct their misbehavior with simply a reminder of the rule.*

Second, the teacher would need to develop with him some alternatives, such as writing down his comments instead of blurting them out, and then coach him to adopt those alternatives. Third, the teacher would need to warn him of the consequences if the behavior continued and follow through with those consequences while sustaining a mutually respectful relationship with him.

Class clowns generate the most disorder when the class is functioning as a whole group, such as during a lecture or **recitation.** Although they seek to dominate during small-group interactions as well, their impact is restricted to that smaller audience. Therefore, teachers with a class clown need to plan more small-group and fewer or shorter whole-class learning activities. *Whenever you have some students monopolizing the class's time, you need to decentralize instruction.*

For example, instead of performing an activity as a demonstration followed by a whole-class discussion, have the students carry out and discuss the activity themselves in small groups. Or, instead of conducting the entire closing summary as a whole class, have each student turn to a neighbor and, as a pair, discuss and list the main points of the lesson. Only the last few minutes might then be a whole-class compilation of the main points.

Note to Ellen's Story: Communicating High Expectations

A teacher's consistently communicating high social expectations can improve students' personal and social development, such as their willingness to cooperate, participate, or collaborate with others.

- Brophy, J. E. (1988). Educating teachers about managing classrooms and students. *Teaching and Teacher Education, 4*(1), 1–18.

Millie's Story

I have 30 ninth graders in my eighth-period math class. One student, Alonzo, was the class clown, trying to monopolize everyone's attention regardless of the activity. To make matters worse, he sat next to his best friend and chatted with him when he wasn't bidding for everyone else's attention.

One day, a straw broke the camel's back. The girl who sat in front of Alonzo spoke to me after class and, with tears in her eyes, reported that he had been throwing spitballs at her, kicking her chair, and poking her in the back for quite some time. When she asked to have her seat changed, I told her that I would move his instead.

Seeing Alonzo before the next class, I told him I was changing his seat. Immediately defensive, denials poured from his lips. "Whaaaat?" he said. "But I haven't done anything wrong!" I calmly responded that if he hadn't done anything, then he had no reason to feel guilty, but I was moving his seat anyway.

Since the move, I have heard no more complaints from the girl, and away from his buddy, Alonzo is less disruptive. His new seat is near the door, and I intend to tell him that the next move, if his disruptions persist, would be to the other side of that door.

Like Danny and Eric, Millie protected her learning environment. However, she solved only part of the problem. How could she, like Ellen, also help her student develop better self-control?

Note: Class Clowns

Class clowns are one category of students who misbehave by persistently seeking attention (see also Chapter 27). Such students feel important only when getting attention. Consequently, reprimands work only temporarily. See Dreikurs et al. (1982) for specific interventions.

- Dreikurs, R., Grundwald, B., & Pepper, F. (1982). *Maintaining sanity in the classroom: Classroom management techniques* (2nd ed.). New York: Harper & Row.

When Students
Are Your Buddies

One challenge for **novice teachers** is conceptualizing their role as a teacher. Many of the roles they adopt, such as parent, police officer, entertainer, preacher, or buddy, just don't work in the classroom. Jedd and Connor each made the mistake of adopting the role of buddy.

Jedd's Story

In the past few weeks, I have become aware of a trend in my classroom. A few students in each class do not take their work seriously. They give trivial answers, chat incessantly, and ask me about homework and other issues as if I weren't in the middle of a lesson. Their behavior has been an ongoing problem. I have moved seats and said repeatedly, "I need you to be quiet right now," but I have had only limited success.

After some reflection, I understood the root of the problem. Unfortunately, it was my own behavior. During my early weeks, I developed a friendly, joking rapport with certain students instead of an appropriate teacher–student relationship. Despite all the warnings about becoming their buddy, I was just that. The students who were disruptive were the ones I had become friendly with.

(Continued)

(Continued)

I have, with effort, been able to resolve the situation, especially because the students have come to realize that I give quizzes, expect homework on time, and otherwise hold them to a high standard. But the message to me was clear: Be aware of the relationship you are establishing with your students. Fewer **discipline problems** arise if you cultivate a teacher–student relationship instead of a buddy–buddy relationship.

Jedd, when telling us that some of his students were not taking their work seriously, said, "Unfortunately, it [the root of the problem] was my own behavior." I would have liked to respond to Jedd, "Fortunately, it was your own behavior, and even more fortunately, you realize it." Rather than blame his students for being silly or rude, he recognized his own contribution to the problem, and as a remedy, upheld his strict standards. *Only when you recognize your own contribution to a problem do you have any power to solve it.*

Connor's Story

Before I began student teaching, I spent a week observing my cooperating teacher's lessons. I would sit in the back of the room with two students, Evan and Jake. During that week, we became friends, talking before and after class about cars, the newest TV programs, and current events.

Finally, I began teaching the class. On the very first day, I was giving a brief lecture. The class was quiet and attentive except for Evan and Jake. I tolerated their chatter for a while but then decided to say something.

"Evan! Jake!"

They looked up at me with grins on their faces.

"The two of you are making me look like a fool. Show me the same respect everyone else is."

Their grins folded into frowns.

> While finishing the lesson, I realized that Evan and Jake had considered me a buddy, one who wouldn't mind their inattentiveness. And I realized that my scolding may have alienated them.
>
> Evan and Jake are reasonable kids. So I asked them to stay after class and talk with me. I suppose they expected a grilling. They were surprised when I apologized for barking at them. They saw, however, that I needed their cooperation. I actually said, "I need your help." Since then, I have had no problem.
>
> I could have easily gone overboard and become a dictator, but I am so glad I didn't. We have benefited so much from a cooperative and mutually respectful relationship.

Like Jedd, Connor recognized his own contribution to his students' **misbehavior.** He went further than Jedd, however. He apologized to Evan and Jake after class. *Don't be afraid to admit your mistakes.*

Connor needed a way to express his anger and reaffirm his expectations without attacking Evan and Jake. He could have said, for example, "I feel like a fool standing here without everyone's attention. I need everyone to show me respect." *To safeguard relationships with their students, teachers need to be careful, especially when angry, to express how they feel without deprecating their students.* In private, however, he did speak to them appropriately when he said, "I need your help." He spoke about his own feelings and needs without criticizing his students, and in doing so, he fostered their self-control. *Rather than impose control, a teacher should foster students' self-control.*

Last, Connor was effective because he demonstrated a willingness to work with Evan and Jake. *A "working with" rather than a "doing to" approach promotes student maturity.*

Both Jedd and Connor struggled with conceptualizing their role, an issue that teachers wrestle with throughout their novice years. Novice teachers tend to see themselves as a parent, warden, intimidator, or dictator on one hand and, when an authoritarian approach doesn't work, as an entertainer, social director, or buddy on the other. In other words, they vacillate between extremes because they have yet to conceptualize the single role they can assume consistently.

How successful have you been conceptualizing your role as a teacher?

Note: Metaphors and Images

The metaphors teachers use to conceptualize their role influence their choice of **classroom management** strategies. Because each metaphor encompasses a set of beliefs, a host of changes can follow the adoption of a new metaphor.

- Tobin, K. (1990). *Metaphors and images in teaching* (What Research Says to the Science and Mathematics Teacher, No. 5). Perth, Western Australia: Curtin University of Technology, The Key Centre for School Science and Mathematics.

During her first year of teaching, Kerrie described her self-image as changing sequentially from mother to community pillar, bitch, policewoman, supervisor, and orchestra conductor.

- Bullough, R. V., Jr. (1989). *First-year teacher: A case study*. New York: Teachers College Press.

17

When You Have a Student Who Talks a Lot

Eight **novice teachers** each tried to cope with one or a few students whose talking during class disrupted the entire lesson. First, each teacher issued a series of pleas or warnings. What did the teacher do next, when that didn't work?

In the first set of two **stories,** each teacher adopted a signal of disapproval. In the second set, each of the two teachers moved one or two students' seats. In the third set, each of the three moved a student's seat but also offered an opportunity for redemption.

Each of these teachers felt the strategy worked. The last story, however, is about a teacher who, alas, made a threat and then felt obliged to carry it out.

SIGNALING DISAPPROVAL

Steve's Story

A couple of weeks ago, I used a technique that worked well for me. I had one student in the back of the classroom who loved to talk. Of course, his talking disrupted the whole back row, causing other students to engage in conversations ranging from local gossip to the final score of the Chicago Bulls game. Well, I knew I had to take care of the situation immediately, that it would only get worse if I didn't.

So I went to the source and said, "Brian, please turn around and pay attention." A few minutes later, I could hear talking around Brian again, so I tried a different technique. I walked closer to Brian, stood there, and said, "I'll wait." In 3 seconds, the room was quiet. And it stayed quiet. Amazed, I continued with the lesson. The "I'll wait" signal has worked for me ever since.

Steve's signal had two phases. First, he moved toward Brian. Sometimes just moving toward the source of disruption is sufficient to prevent or stop it. Called **proximity interference,** it's a useful first step in a management plan because it is nonverbal. *Nonverbal signals are better than verbal signals because they do not provoke defensive arguments or hostile confrontations. Nonverbal signals also do not interrupt the flow of the lesson, and they invite the students to control their own behavior.* The second phase of Steve's signal was to make a brief, almost private statement to Brian and the kids around him. Steve did not preach, moralize, or scold. He simply said, "I'll wait." Thus Steve used a two-phase signal consisting of a nonverbal and then a slightly more intrusive verbal intervention.

If necessary, Steve could have enhanced the effect of his signal by coupling it with a bold stance or resolute expression or gesture, such as folding his arms, and using that set of cues consistently with and exclusively for that signal (see Chapter 6, Jodi's Story). *Teachers can strengthen a signal with multiple cues.* But what could Steve have done if Brian still continued to talk? See the next story for what Merry did.

Merry's Story

As I was about to begin my eighth-period class, I felt the energy vibrate through the room. I told the students to take their seats and settle down. They did what I told them, all of them except Joel. As I started the lesson, he continued to talk and fidget with his back to the front of the room. As the lesson continued, I had to give Joel several direct warnings about his disruptive behavior. My warnings seemed to work but only temporarily. I knew something more had to be done, so I asked Joel to see me after class.

After class, I told Joel how intelligent I thought he was, that I thought he was a "good kid" and that the others looked up to him. I asked him how he felt about school and his teachers. For the most part, his responses were respectful and positive. I told him that changing his behavior would do a world of good, not only for himself but as an example for the class. Both Joel and I left our conversation with a positive outlook for the rest of the year.

The next day, as I started class, Joel was up to his old tricks again, chatting at inappropriate times and misbehaving. I immediately stopped writing on the board, swiftly turned around, and gave him a hard stare. As we made eye contact, he nodded in recognition. Joel seemed to have more self-control after that, needing only a quick glance every now and then to keep him in line.

Merry explained to Joel in private how his behavior was affecting himself and others. *A private conversation preserves the student's or students' dignity, thereby forestalling a defensive or hostile response.* Second, she communicated the high expectations she had for him as an achiever and class leader. *Communicating high expectations is likely to improve student behavior as well as achievement.* Finally, like Steve's proximity interference, Merry used a nonverbal signal, in her case a hard stare, to remind Joel of their discussion and presumably his commitment to improve. *If students have made a commitment to a rule, especially one they had a share in creating, they are likely to correct their **misbehavior** with simply a reminder of the rule.*

MOVING SEATS

Mario's Story

I tried being the nice guy first and then the bad guy, the guy who yells, but neither role worked for me. One student in particular continued to be a perpetual talker.

Normally, he would make only a few comments that were off the wall, but on one particular day, his antics persisted. So I called his name and reassigned him to a seat in the front of the room. He packed his belongings as if he were heading for Outer Mongolia, sulking his way to the vacant desk. But after that, he stopped making off-the-wall comments and has become one of the bright students in the class.

Moving the talkative student to the front row improved both the student's behavior and achievement, the latter quite dramatically. Mario's story, however, suggests he had another problem, that of conceptualizing his role as a teacher (see Chapter 16). Mario, like many novice teachers, vacillated between extremes, in his case between being the nice guy and then the bad guy, instead of finding the single role he could assume consistently. A novice teacher can take a long time to find that role.

Rachel's Story

During one lesson last week, the students were completely out of control. They kept on talking—and their talk wasn't about social studies. No matter what I said or did, I knew I was losing them.

Although the whole class seemed to be talking at first, I saw that only two were engaging the others in conversations. Thinking back to what I had read and advice I had been given, I quickly decided to stop the class and move the two ringleaders. They resisted with groans: "But why?" and "Do I have to?" But I held my position. Then I focused back on the lesson.

What a difference! The students quickly forgot about having to move away from their friends, and the talking ceased. I was able to finish the lesson without much difficulty. By the next day, I didn't even have to remind them where to sit. They just sat in their newly assigned seats.

Rachel determined the dynamics of the group, identified the ringleaders, made a decision, and then executed it firmly. *Execute your decisions with the conviction of a baseball umpire.*

Offering an Opportunity for Redemption

Fred's Story

The other teachers told me Julio might be a **discipline problem.** In fact, he turned out to be a major nuisance and a source of constant noise and disruption. After a few days, I pulled him aside after class and told him that his behavior was becoming intolerable and if I saw him causing or even suspected that he was causing another disturbance, I would move him from the back to the front of the room. Julio was not listening too intently. He was focused on getting away from me.

Two days later, I was giving a quiz, and during the distribution of quiz papers, Julio kept talking to his neighbor. I told him to stop and move to the front. He reluctantly agreed until he realized the change would be permanent. Then he started yelling at me in front of the class. No, he wouldn't sit there, he was not the only one at fault; others had been talking too. My mistake of confronting him publicly became clear, but I also had to save face. So I yelled back. He finally sat down and took the quiz.

Right before class the next day, I pulled him aside in the hall and started discussing the situation with him. Feeling he had been unjustly punished, he became extremely upset.

He had been out to test me, and only now did he realize how serious I had been. But I realized his hating me would only prompt more disruptions. So I gave him a second chance. He promised to improve his behavior, and he did.

Once Fred changed his approach, he was able to foster Julio's cooperation.

Fred's initial approach was to use a threat and a punishment. *Using threats (or bribes) to control student behavior undermines any potential for a mutually respectful relationship.* And *punishment does not deter misbehavior; it fosters resentment, not cooperation.*

Fred's second approach, however, was a "working with" rather than a "doing to" approach. *A "working with" rather than a "doing to" approach promotes student maturity* because it establishes a relationship based on mutual respect rather than one based on domination and compliance. Fred showed Julio that he was willing to give him a second chance, and Julio made a commitment to improve. *The promise of redemption is a strong motivator.* How could you use the promise of redemption to promote a student's cooperation?

During their conversation in the hall, Fred listened to Julio express his feelings of having been unjustly punished. Students' anger can intimidate a novice teacher, but listening to their complaints and acknowledging their feelings is the beginning of a relationship. Perhaps Fred had said something like this to Julio: "I see that this seat change has been a real bummer for you." If so, such a statement would have been vague enough to give Julio an opportunity to express his feelings and precise enough for him to feel understood. *A teacher should be strict about students' behavior but permissive about their feelings.*

Lois's Story

A girl in one of my morning classes insists on talking to her neighbors. Normally, just saying her name is enough to get her to stay quiet for a while. However, on Tuesday, Cindy just wouldn't stay quiet. After a second warning, I switched her seat to the front of the room.

By Wednesday, I could see that the seat change would not be enough. After the first warning, I told Cindy she would have the choice of staying quiet so that she and everyone around her could learn or moving her seat into the hall until she could gain control.

The next time she began to chat, I calmly told her that she had made her choice to sit in the hall.

After several minutes, while the other students were working, I went out into the hall and discussed with Cindy how her behavior was affecting her and her fellow students. Then I allowed her to return to class. Since that day, she has spoken in class only when it's been appropriate.

I realize now that my action on Tuesday to change her seat was not enough. On Wednesday, however, I gave her a choice and followed through with the promised consequence. The discussion we had helped Cindy understand why she needs to control herself.

How did Lois's offering a choice compare with Fred's issuing a threat? They each warned their student and then followed through with the promised consequence. Lois, however, was composed, whereas Fred was agitated. First, unlike Fred, Lois had a systematic plan for dealing with Cindy: She gave Cindy two warnings; then a seat change to the front; followed by another warning coupled with a clear consequence, the seat change to the hall; then a private conference; and finally, redemption. *Teachers need a systematic management plan ranging from subtle to progressively more direct and intrusive interventions.*

Second, Lois explained to Cindy why moving her seat into the hall would be necessary, namely, so that Cindy and everyone else around her could concentrate. Fred, on the other hand, simply told Julio that his behavior was becoming intolerable. *Students need to understand the rationale behind a rule, **routine,** or expectation, that each is not simply an arbitrary attempt to control their behavior.*

Third, Cindy could infer that the seat change would be only temporary, until she could gain control. Remember, Julio became defiant only when he realized his seat change would be permanent. Thus Cindy, unlike Julio, could see the seat change less as a punishment and more as a **time-out,** an opportunity for her, without further consequences, to gain composure before returning to class. To summarize, Lois's offering a choice was more successful than Fred's issuing a threat. *Offering a choice fosters autonomy rather than dependency and lessens defiance.*

Lenora's Story

A few students sit close together and chat with or pass notes to one another. I assigned seats one day for the purpose of doing group work. I shuffled the deck a little, but my main objective was to put some students near those they could help.

I intentionally left together a pair of students who seemed friendly with one another. Marge was doing well on quizzes, and Helen needed to improve. The group work went well, but the next day—I'd kept the same seating arrangement—Marge and Helen disruptively engaged in their own conversation. I walked over to Helen as I continued to speak to the class. I tapped lightly on her desk and quietly asked her to face forward and continue with her notebook entries.

Some minutes later, Helen, Marge, and now Joanne as well were engaged in a conversation. Again I positioned myself at Helen's desk, the hub of the activity, this time whispering for her to move to a desk a few rows away from the temptation to turn and talk. Then, after engaging the class in a new task, I walked over to Helen and asked her whether she understood why I'd asked her to move. She had understood and explained my message clearly. She asked whether she could sit by Marge tomorrow, and I said, "As long as you understand the behavior expected of you and feel you can handle it, you may sit next to Marge."

I think I managed the situation well. I focused on correcting Helen without disrupting the lesson, I didn't raise my voice, and I provided her with an opportunity to control her own behavior without having to brood over teacher unfairness.

Like Lois, Lenora had a systematic management plan. She began with proximity interference, walking over to Helen. Then she used **touch interference,** light physical contact with an object near Helen, in this case Helen's desk.

Next, she discreetly asked Helen to desist. Only after these steps failed did she whisper to Helen to move so as to avoid further temptation.

And, like Lois, Lenora had additional steps in her management plan. After telling Helen to move, she checked to see whether Helen understood why Lenora had moved her. *A teacher needs to make sure that students understand the problem from the teacher's perspective and that he or she understands it from theirs.* Last, Lenora offered Helen an opportunity for redemption.

Throughout the execution of her management plan, Lenora provided repeated opportunities for Helen to practice self-control. Nevertheless, Lenora maintained her focus on the lesson and understood the importance of maintaining that focus. *For every minute you divert your students from the course of your lesson, you will lose several times that amount trying to reengage them.*

Managing the behavior of a disruptive student is necessarily a long-range undertaking, requiring weeks if not months to establish a mutually respectful relationship. Which strategies or combinations of strategies in these eight stories would be likely to promote long-range success for you?

Note to Steve's and Lenora's Stories: Proximity Interference

Levin and Nolan (2007) recommend using proximity interference when **signal interference** doesn't work, that is, when the disruptive student does not respond to eye contact, the teacher's pointing, or other discreet but definite signals. If proximity interference does not curb the misbehavior, then they recommend touch interference, the next step in their hierarchy of interventions.

- Levin, J., & Nolan, J. F. (2007). *Principles of classroom management: A professional decision-making model* (5th ed.). Boston: Allyn & Bacon.

Making a Threat

Barry's Story

Today I had a problem while giving a test. I repeatedly asked for quiet for those students still working. It felt like a slap in the face when a few students ignored my request. So I calmly stated that the next person to talk would receive a zero. Not one second later, a student decided to test whether I had the resolve to follow through. He turned around in his seat and started talking to another student. So I stated in a firm but calm voice, "Charles, zero. Please give me your test." He did so, and I marked a zero on his test. Most of the class could not believe what I had done.

I really had not directed my earlier requests for quiet toward Charles. Other students had been talking. His blatant disregard of my order, however, forced me to give him the zero. I had backed myself into a corner. If I had not handed out the zero, the talking would have continued, and it would have disrupted other students. I had taken a stand that I had to enforce. I must be careful not to back myself into a corner again.

Barry needed to have planned an independent activity for his students to do upon finishing their test. *Unstructured time generates boredom, restlessness, and disruption.* And because he had no systematic plan to manage the disruption, he responded spontaneously with a threat he felt he had to enforce. How could you rewrite Barry's Story after the second sentence so he would be more likely to be successful?

When a Group Misbehaves (or Is Likely to Misbehave)

Three **novice teachers** each solve the problem of a group misbehaving or likely to misbehave during a learning activity. In the first **story**, Dora reacts to the **misbehavior.** In the second, Larry forestalls it. And in the third, Tina does both, first reacting to the misbehavior and then forestalling its recurrence.

Dora's Story

The four boys who sit together in the back row are a challenging blend of academic aversion, disciplinary history (one wears a bracelet and is on house arrest), and raging hormones. On any given day, at least one of them is usually absent, a circumstance that greatly diminishes their toxicity but hinders my quest for a solution. I have, however, tried two approaches.

(Continued)

(Continued)

I call my first approach Divide and Conquer. To move even one of them away from the others renders the rest of them powerless. But alas! This is a class of 31 students in a classroom with only 30 seats. Moving one of them means putting a gentler soul among the remaining three. No one would relish going there.

I call my second approach Hitting the Nail on the Head. I call all four (or the worst of the four) up to my desk, and speaking in a whisper so only they can hear, I say, "If I have to speak to any of you again, I am prepared to write a letter home about how your behavior has been obstructing your academic progress." When they call my bluff, I immediately produce the draft of such a letter, and they quickly back down. I follow this strategy with Divide and Conquer.

I tried other strategies first, namely, the usual nonverbal strategies of moving closer to them, tapping on their desks, or staring directly at them while shaking my head, but those strategies have failed to work. The consequence of a letter home, however, holds them at bay. They have learned that I mean what I say.

Teachers need a systematic management plan ranging from subtle to progressively more direct and intrusive interventions. Dora relied on such a plan beginning with nonverbal strategies and culminating in giving the boys the choice between complying and facing the consequence. But her strategies were strictly reactive. A **reactive management strategy** is designed to stop or punish a threat to or actual breach of order. On the other hand, a **proactive management strategy** is designed to prevent the threat or breach altogether. *Proactive management strategies are better than reactive management strategies.* Novice teachers, so consumed with the immediacy of their disciplinary challenges, are likely, however, to overlook proactive strategies and concentrate exclusively on reactive strategies.

An example of a proactive strategy for Dora would be her conferring with the boys so they understood the problem from her perspective and she understood it from theirs. *A teacher needs to make sure that students understand the problem from the teacher's perspective and that he or she understands it from theirs.*

Then she could have asked them how she could help to make the lessons more meaningful for them. *Teachers are more likely to be successful with students who see the teacher as on their side.*

Nevertheless, she ultimately would need them to take responsibility for their behavior and make a commitment to change. While offering them support, she would still need to warn them of the consequence if they didn't improve, such as her forbidding them to participate in an activity.

Another example of a proactive strategy for Dora would be her planning more small-group activities, in which the four would be separated from each other, and fewer whole-class activities, such as lectures, demonstrations, and **recitations.** *Whenever you have some students monopolizing the class's time, you need to decentralize instruction.*

Dora's strategies were not only reactive, but the choice she offered them was really a threat, not a choice. *Using threats (or bribes) to control student behavior undermines any potential for a mutually respectful relationship.* An example of offering them a real choice would have been for her to say, "Every day, you have a choice. You can either participate cooperatively in our activities or each of you can separate from the others, sit by yourself, and get credit for the lesson by outlining the pertinent pages in the textbook." *Offering a choice fosters autonomy rather than dependency and lessens defiance.* Instead of threatening to send a letter to their parents, Dora, by giving them a real choice, would be communicating to the boys that she, not their parents, is the authority in the classroom and that they are responsible directly to her.

How could Dora use other proactive strategies to treat the problem?

Larry's Story

I have two disruptive students in an eighth-grade physical science class. The purpose of one of our lessons was to learn how to calculate speed. The students were to work in pairs to design, construct, and

(Continued)

(Continued)

launch a paper airplane. Then one member of the class would time the flight from liftoff to crash landing of each pair's airplane, and another would measure the flight distance so every pair could calculate its airplane's speed.

At first glance, this activity might seem easy to pull off, but when you introduce two students who would do anything to disrupt the learning environment, you can see that the entire lesson was at risk. So how could I prevent their spoiling the lesson?

I gave them each a leadership position to make them feel important and have a presence in the classroom, which is what they had been trying to accomplish anyway. I gave them the two big jobs, timekeeper and distance measurer, and told them I knew they could do a great job and I was counting on them. In other words, I used their personalities to our mutual advantage.

Larry used two proactive strategies to forestall the pair's misbehavior. He assigned each of them a leadership position to redirect their behavior, and he expressed high expectations to promote that redirection. *Communicating high expectations is likely to improve behavior as well as achievement.* Larry was successful at least for the short term because he executed his lesson with management as well as curricular objectives in mind. *A teacher needs to consider both management and curricular objectives when planning and executing a lesson.*

Tina's Story

I took my geometry students outside to use similar right triangles to calculate the height of the flagpole. The first three classes went well. The students understood the concepts and cooperated. It was difficult to keep an eye on all the students, but they worked efficiently. My eighth-period class, however, was different.

After I introduced the lesson, we ventured outside. About 5 minutes later, I noticed a group of four students—my students, mind you—playing around on the far side of the building. I immediately felt betrayed, angry that they had taken advantage of me. But I took control of myself and then walked over to them and told them their behavior was unacceptable. Of course, they immediately spouted a list of excuses, but I told them the issue was not up for discussion and they needed to join the others.

All the students eventually finished the activity, and when most of them seemed to understand the concepts, we headed inside. Still, I knew I needed to talk to that group. So I took the four aside and told them that (a) I didn't appreciate their taking advantage of the situation, (b) they are not to work together anymore, and (c) the matter was closed. To my surprise, they agreed without hesitation. I breathed a huge sigh of relief, but the encounter exhausted me physically as well as emotionally.

From this event, I learned that sometimes teachers need to be actors. We need to hide our emotions, be tough, and set the boundaries. Well, I did just that. I acted like I was in charge. If I hadn't, they'd still be testing me.

Tina was necessarily reactive to her group's mischief initially, but she became proactive when she took the four aside later and prohibited them from working together again. This consequence was not a punishment, however. *Punishment does not deter misbehavior; it fosters resentment, not cooperation.* Rather, she was preventing a recurrence and providing an opportunity for each of them to practice better judgment.

Tina, unlike Dora, presented herself to the four as the authority. *Novice teachers have difficulty claiming their power as the authority,* some, perhaps including Tina, feeling awkward at assuming this unfamiliar role. Nevertheless, she composed herself, summoned her courage, and spoke to the group calmly, courteously, briefly, and firmly. You too can *execute your decisions with the conviction of a baseball umpire.* Authority figures do not rant, plead, preach, or belittle; they don't have to.

They *address the situation, not the shortcomings of the student(s).* Thus Tina could sustain a mutually respectful relationship with her students despite having to express disapproval and impose a consequence.

Like Dora, Tina spoke to her students in private. *A private conversation preserves the student's or students' dignity, thereby forestalling a defensive or hostile response.* Thus her students, mindful that she was in charge and grateful for her even-handedness, agreed to her conditions readily.

How could you use Tina's proactive strategy to treat a current problem? How could you use other proactive strategies?

Note: Proactive and
Reactive Management Strategies

Levin and Nolan (2007) recommend seven proactive management strategies to minimize the likelihood of misbehavior. Some examples are changing the pace of the lesson, temporarily removing a distracting object, and redirecting the behavior of off-task students. The goal of proactive management strategies is to encourage students to exercise self-control. The teacher can then treat the misbehaviors that do emerge with reactive management strategies.

- Levin, J., & Nolan, J. F. (2007). *Principles of classroom management: A professional decision-making model* (5th ed.). Boston: Allyn & Bacon.

When a Student Is Outspoken

How did six **novice teachers** respond to each of their students' outspoken remarks? Some of the remarks were public, some private. Some seem to have been unintentionally impertinent, pedantic, or thoughtless, whereas others were probably intentionally impudent, callous, or disparaging. In all cases, the student caught the teacher by surprise. How would you have responded?

Sheila's Story

As the first class was about to begin, I noticed that one of the students—it turned out to be Alan—was staring at me, and after a few minutes, he said, "You remind me of someone."

Fearing where such a conversation could lead, my immediate reaction was to pretend I had not heard him, but I noticed everyone looking at me waiting for a response. So I decided to hold my breath and casually ask, "Oh, really? Who?"

He responded, "My aunt. She's short just like you."

(Continued)

(Continued)

A girl sitting next to him protested, and before I could respond, she ordered Alan to walk up to me, took off her shoes, and said, "Look! I'm short. She is not short!"

Alan turned red in the face and said, "I didn't mean she is as short as you. I just meant that she is short!"

I couldn't help but laugh. One can never predict what these kids will say. Alan has become my protector trying to calm the class whenever the noise level gets out of control. This event is a reminder to me that a teacher needs to have a sense of humor and not take things personally.

Sheila enjoyed the candor of her students.

Erin's Story

As I began to give the notes for Chapter 33, Janet raised her hand, and with a smirk on her face, said, "'Fishes' isn't a word." I told her that although it sounds funny and is not normally used, the textbook uses the term so that's why I used it.

Janet replied, "Well, I'm sorry, but ever since I was little, my parents have told me there's no such word as 'fishes.' We don't call a herd of deer 'deers' either."

I simply said that I was sorry she felt that way and continued giving notes.

As the students were writing, I checked the textbook and announced to the class, "Just so nobody loses any sleep tonight, you can find the word 'fishes' on pages 251–255."

As I thought about it, I wondered whether Janet felt that my remark about not losing sleep had been sarcastic. I know she did not mean to be argumentative. I meant only to clarify why I was using such an uncommon word. Since then, I have become sensitive to the feelings of my students, even if they express themselves rudely, and am careful about the way I phrase my comments to them.

Erin understood that sarcasm poisons relationships. Had she realized before the class was over that Janet might have taken offense, she could have spoken to her or to the entire class, saying something like this:

> You know, I listened to my remark about your not losing sleep over the correct plural for "fish" and began to wonder whether I sounded sarcastic. A sarcastic remark is a mocking remark. Sarcastic remarks are hurtful. So I hope I didn't sound that way, but if I did, I did not intend to, and I am sorry for not having thought more carefully before I spoke.

Don't be afraid to admit your mistakes.

Shannon's Story

As a novice teacher, I have had many **classroom management** issues. Still, one **story** stands out in my mind. One boy in particular tried to get away with everything and really grated on my nerves. I had a hard time with him because I couldn't stomach his obnoxious attitude! But in the beginning, I had ignored his behavior. I know that wasn't the best solution, but that was all I could do without saying something I might regret later.

Just as I started wondering what to do about him, he happened to be absent for a stretch, giving me the opportunity to establish myself with the others. Soon I became comfortable with my classes, and my confidence increased. So when he returned, I was ready for him.

He began the class by hanging over my shoulder while I was helping another student. As I looked up at him, I said, "Can I help you?"

"I'll take this side of the classroom, you take the other side, and we'll both help the students," he replied.

Looking at him directly, I said, "You've been absent for a long time and have a lot of work to make up."

"Well, that is why I'm here. I'm waiting for you to tell me what to do."

(Continued)

(Continued)

I then told him that all he had needed to do was ask me that in the first place. But he promptly replied, "Look, you're the woman, and I'm the man, and the woman follows the orders of the man."

Well, as soon as those words came out of his mouth, I put my foot down. I sternly told him that I didn't need to tolerate his impudence and I wouldn't tolerate it. If he didn't want to work and be in this class, then he could leave now and not come back because I didn't have a problem with his not being there.

Amazingly, my response worked. His eyes popped out of his head, and he immediately said he wanted to do his work and would I please help him with his assignments. I told him I would gladly help him, that all he had to do was ask me respectfully.

Since that day, I have had no problem with him. I believe he respected me for putting my foot down and had wanted me to do that from the very beginning. Now that he knows I am in charge, he is ready to work when he comes to class.

Although Shannon had initially ignored his impudence, she eventually did assert her authority. *Novice teachers have difficulty claiming their power as the authority.* She rebuked him (presumably while keeping the discussion private). *A penetrating comment may be necessary to remind students when they are not living up to expectations or their responsibilities.* She also, however, assured him of her help as long as he asked her respectfully. Moreover, she came to realize her own contribution to the problem, that she should have reproved him earlier. *Only when you recognize your own contribution to a problem do you have any power to solve it.*

How would you have responded to him when you first found his attitude obnoxious?

Victoria's Story

Having been born in Russia, I was aware of my accent. Although I didn't feel comfortable talking about it with my students, I expected to hear comments and questions about it. I heard nothing about it, however, until one day, when I heard a lot.

I started the lesson with my usual **do-now,** review questions about the previous lesson. When we began going over the questions, I heard two girls in the back of the room burst out laughing.

"Mitten what?" one of them asked.

"Mitochondria," I responded.

"I do not understand you, and I can't even hear you!" shouted the other girl. The comment was harsh especially from someone who had been actively participating during our lessons.

The girls kept laughing. Other students picked up on the joke and went along with the girls. I was losing control. I wasn't prepared to discuss my origins with the class that day, but now I had to. I told them I wasn't born in America, related some of my English-learning experiences, and explained the importance of accepting people from other cultures.

I learned that children can sense a teacher's insecurities and that I had to accept and be open about who I am. I also realized that many seventh graders do not understand the experience of being an immigrant in America.

Victoria turned an event that was uncomfortable for her into a learning experience for her students. Like Victoria, you too should *resist the tendency to take your students' misbehaviors personally.* Instead of scolding the girls for their rudeness, Victoria spoke candidly about herself. *Honest communication is fundamental to your relationships with your students.*

Teachers can, however, also teach their students to express themselves thoughtfully. They can, in private, give their students specific and immediate feedback on their behavior. *Students need specific and immediate feedback to recognize their behavior.* For example, Victoria could have said to the girls, "I heard you laughing as we were going over the questions. I knew you were laughing at me, and I felt embarrassed."

Next, Victoria would need to help them see how their behavior affected not only her but the other students. Last, she could help them develop alternative ways of expressing their confusion. For example, she could coach them (and perhaps all her students) to signal when they can't understand her so she could write the words on the board.

Gina's Story

The event occurred during the first few weeks of school. I overheard a student harshly criticizing my teaching. The course is challenging for most of these students, and I can understand his frustration and why he wanted to lash out at me.

I didn't respond in anger. Instead, I simply asked to speak with him at a convenient time. When we met, I said, "I can understand that this class can frustrate you, and like you, I am learning as I go along. I make mistakes in presenting the material, and if I don't explain a concept adequately, I would be glad to help you one-on-one if I can."

Since then, the student has begun to participate in class.

Like Victoria, Gina resisted the tendency to take her student's hostility personally. *Welcome the expression of your students' feelings as feedback to improve your teaching.* Instead, she validated his feelings and offered him help. *A "working with" rather than a "doing to" approach promotes student maturity.*

Note to Gina's Story: Teacher Competence

Students regard a teacher as competent when he or she can explain course concepts clearly. They respect, like, and are motivated to learn with such a teacher. Conversely, they dislike and misbehave for a teacher who confuses them.

- Kounin, J. S. (1970). *Discipline and group management in classrooms.* New York: Holt, Rinehart & Winston.
- Tanner, L. N. (1978). *Classroom discipline for effective teaching and learning.* New York: Holt, Rinehart & Winston.

Colleen's Story

A boy in the back of the room asked, "What are you, stupid?" I honestly think he didn't expect me to hear him. A girl, also in the back, had been asking me a question, and I had had to ask her to repeat it twice because my ears were clogged from a weeklong head cold.

The boy was shocked to find out that I had heard him and immediately put his head down and apologized. Still, I confronted him about his behavior and the 5-week progress report coming up. He must have apologized at least three more times. I concluded by saying that I would never call any of my students stupid.

Other teachers said I should have written him up [referred him to the assistant principal for disciplinary action] right then and there. Upon reflection, however, I think I should have spoken to him after class. Then I would have been better prepared to deal with him calmly.

Both Gina and Colleen happened to overhear each of their student's hostile remarks. Unlike Gina, Colleen took her student's hostility personally, confronted him publicly, and continued to reprimand him, extending the scope of the reprimand even after he had apologized. Upon reflection, however, she realized she should have spoken to him after class, when her anger presumably would have subsided. *Teachers need to be the model of a rational, temperate, consistent, and positive adult, the only such model some of their students may ever see.*

Colleen, instead of exacerbating his humiliation, could have helped him in class to save face. When she heard his remark, she could have explained, "Yes, I feel stupid today. I have such a bad cold. My ears are clogged, and my brain feels half dead. A cold is such a drag." *Good discipline is achieved only through repeated kindnesses.*

When a Student Does Little or No Schoolwork

Three **novice teachers** each responded to a student who had been doing little or no schoolwork. Some students who do little or no schoolwork are passive; others are disruptive. Some can't do the work; others can but won't. Luke's **Story** is about a passive student who wouldn't do the work. Wilma's Story is about a disruptive student who also wouldn't do the work. Jeremy's Story is about a disruptive student who couldn't do the work.

Luke's Story

After giving a short lecture on the genres of fiction, I handed out a worksheet for the students to match each genre to an appropriate story synopsis. One boy in the front of the room, Greg, pushed the worksheet away, saying, "I can't do this." Then he folded his arms and laid his head down on the desk. This unwillingness to complete or even attempt an assignment is typical for him.

The rest of the students finished their worksheets, and as I began to collect them, I wondered what to say to Greg. Then it came to me.

I told him to put his name on the paper. When he asked why, I told him, "Because I have to keep track of the work you do in here." He reluctantly put his name on the sheet.

That night I made sure to correct the worksheets so I could hand them back the next day. I wanted to show Greg that his lack of effort would be reflected in his grade. I put a large zero at the top of his paper and handed it back to him. Later that period, he came up to ask me whether he could do the work to erase the zero. I said yes.

This was the first time I had been able to motivate him. The outcome was gratifying. I learned that students' promptly seeing the consequences of their actions is a great motivator.

Luke's strategy had three phases. First, he told Greg that he was holding him accountable for the assignment. *A penetrating comment may be necessary to remind students when they are not living up to expectations or their responsibilities.* Second, he gave the students, and especially Greg, prompt feedback on their performance. *Students are most receptive to feedback immediately after they complete a task.* And third, he gave Greg the opportunity to resubmit the assignment. *The promise of redemption is a strong motivator.*

Fortunately, Luke had not punished Greg beyond giving him the standard grade for failing to complete an assignment. And fortunately, Greg asked to resubmit the assignment. If he had not asked, Luke would have had to remind Greg of his responsibility and assign him a time, either during or after school, to come in to complete the work. On the other hand, knowing Greg, Luke should have been monitoring him during class, prompting him to use his time productively, and Luke should begin monitoring him now and continue to do so until Greg completes his work regularly.

Wilma's Story

My connection to Carl D. has been weak at best. He is the least motivated student in the class, has not been doing his work, and has been constantly disruptive.

(Continued)

(Continued)

One day, I called on another student named Carl, Carl F., and Carl D. got confused. I explained to him that I had called on Carl F., and Carl D. suggested that I call him by another name, the name Paul, to minimize the confusion. I thought this request was a little strange, but I went along with it.

Actually, his request has been a blessing. By calling him Paul, I have made a strong connection with him. He has been participating more actively in class and is more willing to do his work.

I have also taken to using the names as a warning system. When he misbehaves once, I correct him using the name Paul, but when he pushes too far, I use his real name, mentioning that his behavior flustered me so much that I called him Carl instead of Paul. At this point, he usually exerts more self-control.

Wilma's calling him Paul made Carl feel significant. *Enhancing chronically disruptive students' feelings of significance might, over time, improve their behavior.* She reverted to the name Carl as a more intrusive reminder when, after correcting him as Paul, his **misbehavior** continued. That is, she had a systematic plan to manage his behavior. *Teachers need a systematic management plan ranging from subtle to progressively more direct and intrusive interventions.*

How could you enhance a chronically disruptive student's feelings of significance? Consider assigning the student a high-status role in maintaining the classroom. For example, ask him or her to distribute materials, set up equipment, or create displays. Or consider expressing pleasure at his or her participation in a school event. Say, for example, "I enjoyed seeing you on the soccer field yesterday."

Jeremy's Story

Since the first day of class, Kevin has turned in hardly any assignments, and when he has, they have been incomplete. Furthermore, he hasn't completed any of the earth science lab reports required to sit for the Regents Exam. In fact, he flatly refuses to do any work whatsoever!

His behavior? Well, that's downright awful too. He is disrespectful, talks out during class, and bothers the other students. Several have even told him to leave them alone because they want to participate and need to concentrate.

I have tried various strategies including moving his seat to the front of the room, calling his guardian, and writing referrals, but nothing seems to work. Although his talking out during class has eased somewhat, he continues to keep his head down on the desk throughout the entire lesson, regardless of what I say to him.

Finally, because of numerous suspensions, he has been in our classroom a total of only 10 days since school began 6 weeks ago. How can I make Kevin do his work while teaching the 30 other students?

No one can make Kevin do his work. Unlike Greg and Carl, who wouldn't do the work, Kevin probably can't. He has missed too many classes. Jeremy would need to hold a series of remedial sessions with Kevin to treat both his academic deficiencies and his disruptive behavior, which interact to propel him toward failure.

First, Jeremy would need to have a private conversation with Kevin to express concern more for his welfare than for his completing his work and to suggest to him a series of remedial sessions. Second, Kevin would need to make the choice between making the commitment to change and having to repeat the course. *Offering a choice fosters autonomy rather than dependency and lessens defiance.*

During the sessions, Jeremy would need to point out to Kevin his academic progress and help him understand how his behavior has been undermining his peers' acceptance. And third, Jeremy would need to coach Kevin to adopt more appropriate ways to express his feelings. *The development of a trusting relationship with a caring adult is the most effective strategy for treating a student with a chronic school problem.*

Note: Cycle of Discouragement

Greg, Carl, and Kevin may each be caught in a **cycle of discouragement.** That is, given their history of academic failure, they may misbehave as a way to feel significant. The consequences, however, result in a reaffirmation of their sense of failure and their need to misbehave further. To break the cycle, a teacher, in addition to stopping the misbehavior, would have to find a positive way to fulfill their need to feel significant (Levin & Nolan, 2007). How could you help one of your students feel more significant?

- Levin, J., & Nolan, J. F. (2007). *Principles of classroom management: A professional decision-making model* (5th ed.). Boston: Allyn & Bacon.

Kevin may have the added problem of being unable to do the work. Grabe (1985) would, therefore, recommend a **mastery learning** approach to break his cycle of discouragement. Mastery learning is an instructional approach in which students are individually given the time and support to master a set of concepts or skills at their current academic level before progressing to the next level. With this approach, Kevin would have the opportunity, with diligence, to catch up to his peers.

- Grabe, M. (1985). Attributions in a mastery instructional system: Is an emphasis on effort harmful? *Contemporary Educational Psychology, 10*, 113–126.

21

When a Student Seems Troubled

Two **novice teachers** each face their own disappointment when dealing with a student who seemed troubled. If you too have been disappointed, consider whether your disappointment, like Harry's and Mitchell's, was based on an unrealistic expectation.

Harry's Story

When I started student teaching a few weeks ago, I saw that a certain boy had not been working well with my cooperating teacher. She explained that the boy had been disrespectful at the beginning of the school year, and when she addressed him about it, he got offended and remained distant.

Then, when I started working as a volunteer assistant coach for the track team, I got to see this boy in a different setting. As one of the runners, he seemed to connect with me. My cooperating teacher was impressed with the trust he seemed to have in me.

Any trust we might have shared ended this past week. He turned in an essay in which he had used several vulgar words. Shocked, I knew I had to speak to him about it. When I finally spoke to him, I told him he had to redo the assignment and was going to lose points.

(Continued)

(Continued)

I thought he would understand and accept this outcome graciously. Instead, he couldn't understand what the big deal was. He has not resubmitted the essay and tries to make me uncomfortable with persistent sarcastic remarks. I guess I misjudged the relationship we had. I was disappointed, to say the least.

Harry might not have misjudged their relationship. He simply didn't realize how fragile the relationship with a troubled youngster can be. Instead of telling the boy he had to redo the essay, Harry should have offered him the choice to redo it. *Offering a choice fosters autonomy rather than dependency and lessens defiance.* Harry could have framed their conversation as an opportunity for the boy to improve his writing skills and thereby gain more points. Then, by making a distinction between street talk and classroom talk, Harry could have shown him how, by using the appropriate language, the boy could create a more precise and persuasive essay. *A "working with" rather than a "doing to" approach promotes student maturity.*

Note to Harry's Story:
Choices and Moral Development

Giving students control, that is, responsibility for making decisions including choices, fosters their moral development because they have an opportunity to construct and reflect on their values (Kohn, 2006a).

- Kohn, A. (2006a). *Beyond discipline: From compliance to community, 10th anniversary edition.* Alexandria, VA: Association for Supervision and Curriculum Development.

According to Piaget (1965) and later, Kohlberg (e.g., 1969), children progress through stages of moral development. For example, most teenagers are at the stage in which they can begin to connect an action to its consequences.

- Kohlberg, L. (1969). *Stages in the development of moral thought and action*. New York: Holt, Rinehart & Winston.
- Piaget, J. (1965). *The moral judgment of the child*. New York: Free Press.

Mitchell's Story

In mid-February, I assigned a one-paragraph, in-class writing assignment to complete our study of the landscape regions of the world. I asked the students to explain why they would each choose to live in a particular region.

One student started off with a great response. Choosing the mountains, he correctly identified the characteristics of the region and then added that he would be able to "pick out a perfect place to commit suicide." I read his essay pretty late at night—it was one of the last ones I had to read—and I was shocked.

This boy has a tendency to be inappropriate and goof off, and his behavior, sadly, has made him an outcast among his peers. If he was joking around, then he needed to realize how serious the issue of teen suicide is. If he was earnest, then he needed help, and I was frightened for him. So I spoke with the boy's guidance counselor who, agreeing that the matter was serious, said he would meet that day to speak first with the boy and then with the school psychologist.

The boy was pulled out of my sixth-period class and returned 15 minutes later. I overheard him talking to another student as they were leaving the room at the end of class. He said, "Mr._____ thought I was serious when I wrote yesterday about committing suicide. . . ." That was all I heard. I must admit I was relieved to hear that his paragraph was some kind of sick joke, but I was also angry that he would have written something like that, angry that I cared and that he hadn't realized the impact his joke could have on somebody.

The next day, I followed up with the staff. The guidance counselor said that the boy didn't know why he wrote it, that it was just a joke. Neither the counselor nor the school psychologist seemed to be concerned about the boy's emotional state. Again, I was relieved.

(Continued)

(Continued)

But I still have some lingering anger. I am pleased with how quickly the staff investigated the threat but disappointed that they seemed less concerned than I. And I wish I had taken the opportunity to speak with the boy about the seriousness of teen suicide. Finally, a part of me remains afraid for this boy as I continue to wonder why he wrote that.

Mitchell responded as the law requires, by reporting the threat to someone in charge, whether it be the school nurse, principal, or guidance counselor. Beyond that, Mitchell could have done little else. He simply does not have the expertise. *Teachers need to recognize and accept their limitations.* Aside from observing the boy regularly for other threatening signs, however, Mitchell might make an occasion to speak with him, not so much about the seriousness of teen suicide but to coach him on gaining social acceptance.

Both Harry and Mitchell were disappointed. Harry was disappointed in the relationship he had made with his student, and Mitchell was disappointed in the school's apparently perfunctory response to the suicide threat. Each had an unrealistic expectation, a common source of disappointment for novice teachers. How have you been disappointed by an expectation?

When Students Bully

Four **novice teachers** each believed that students must show their classmates respect, but none of them had confidence in their response to **bullying,** that is, a form of physical, psychological, or social violence in which a group or individual targets for abuse the person or property of another group or individual perceived as vulnerable.

Vera's Story

As my students were getting into groups to identify examples of different figures of speech, I noticed that one of the groups was excluding Holden. Holden is new to the school and has difficulty learning. The kids in his group were not only excluding him but making fun of him as well. I still don't know exactly what they said to him, but I moved him to a different group right away.

Once I got him settled in his new group, I went over to the kids who had been disrespectful to him and said in a low, stern voice, "I will not tolerate your making fun of anyone in this classroom, and if you do it again, I will refer you for disciplinary action." They knew I was serious.

(Continued)

(Continued)

I am not sure whether I was too harsh, but I remember being made fun of in junior high. I recall the incident and even the kids who made fun of me. I feel that too few teachers discipline students for that kind of behavior. I hope I never have to refer any of my kids, but I want them to know that they must show their classmates respect.

Recognizing her responsibility to provide a **socially and psychologically safe learning environment,** Vera intervened swiftly to rebuke the group, briefly identifying both the offense and the punishment for a repeat violation. *A penetrating comment may be necessary to remind students when they are not living up to expectations or their responsibilities.* However, she rebuked them in private. *A private conversation preserves the student's or students' dignity, thereby forestalling a defensive or hostile response.*

Yet Vera wondered whether she had been too harsh. On the contrary, her rebuke, though necessary, was insufficient. She also needed to teach the students why their behavior was unacceptable and how they could make amends. After class, she needed to explain to them first the difference between feelings and behavior, that, yes, they have feelings but not the right to act on them. For example, she could have said, "I know you don't want him in your group, but you may not exclude him. He has as much right to participate in the group as you do."

Vera also needed to explain how their behavior was a violation of the Golden Rule. And finally, she needed to express her confidence in their abilities to control their behavior and her hope that they would apologize to Holden. In short, warning them of a punishment was necessary, but she also needed to work with them to improve their attitude toward Holden. *A "working with" rather than a "doing to" approach promotes student maturity.*

> ## Ollie's Story
>
> One event that particularly bothers me is when one student taunts another. On a few occasions, I have noticed such taunts directed at a certain Asian boy who has difficulty speaking English. I had held back from addressing these insults but regretted my inaction and began to watch for an opportunity to step in. A week or so later, a different boy taunted someone, this time about being a homosexual.
>
> I started to lay into this boy really hard, raising my voice and carrying on for about half a minute. Then I suddenly noticed the other students staring at me in astonishment. I suppose they never thought I would castigate a student like that, especially in front of the whole class. In retrospect, I wish I hadn't.
>
> Quickly addressing the inappropriateness of the remark and having him stay after class to discuss the matter privately would have been the better alternative. Having gotten caught up in the spontaneous events of the classroom, I failed to recognize an issue that could have been handled better privately.

Unlike Vera's, Ollie's rebuke was both public and judgmental. All he accomplished was to humiliate the bully (and perhaps the victim) and demonstrate his own lack of self-control. *Teachers need to be the model of a rational, temperate, consistent, and positive adult, the only such model some of their students may ever see.*

Ollie may have overreacted to offset his earlier inaction. Novices often vacillate between extremes as they struggle to find a temperate response. Ollie, however, needed to express his anger without judging his student's character. *To safeguard relationships with their students, teachers need to be careful, especially when angry, to express how they feel without deprecating their students.* For example, he could say, "I get upset when I hear one student mock another. We are here to help not hurt one another." In other words, *instead of criticizing the actions of their students, teachers can safely express their anger by referring to their own feelings.*

Sam's Story

I was eliciting a response to this question: "Have you ever seen 100,000,000,000 of anything?" With his hand waving, I called on Gil, who said, "Yeah, dirt!"

Incredulous, I asked, "You've seen 100 billion dirts?"

"Yeah, every day on Marvin's clothes."

Gil was referring to a classmate documented as neglected at home. Several students had asked me to change their seat because of Marvin's offensive odor.

The kids were now looking at me to see how I would respond, whether I would laugh along with them. I needed to defuse the tension immediately before the abuse escalated so I sent Gil out into the hall to wait for me while I elicited a more appropriate response to my question. Meanwhile, I could see that Marvin was hurt, but I wasn't sure how to protect him. I displayed some notes on the overhead projector and told the class that Gil was in big trouble and that I would be returning momentarily to what had better be a quiet classroom.

I spoke to Gil in the hallway. "Do you realize that what you said was inappropriate?"

"But it's true."

"How do you think Marvin feels?"

"I don't care about Marvin."

"Does your mom take care of you? Does she draw your bath or wash your clothes?"

"Yeah," Gil conceded.

"Well, Marvin has to do these things on his own."

"I don't care."

I couldn't understand why I wasn't getting through to Gil. He has instigated minor disruptions but always respected my authority. I was disappointed in him and decided to tell him so.

"Gil, I've just learned something about you. You are cruel. You hurt his feelings in front of the whole class, and you don't even care. From now on, whenever I look at you, I'm going to remember how you behaved today." Then Gil cracked, finally showing remorse, but not for having hurt Marvin, rather, for having lost his status with me.

I believe I acted correctly in getting Gil out of the classroom and explaining to him why what he did was wrong. Also, I kept the two boys after class so Gil could apologize to Marvin. But I should not have told Gil that he is cruel. Instead, I should have said that he had done a cruel thing. And I should have provided a way for him to regain his status with me.

Sam intervened swiftly to speak privately with Gil to make sure he was aware of his behavior and how it affected Marvin. Sam, however, like Ollie, needed to *address the situation, not the shortcomings of the student(s)*. Instead of judging Gil, as he did with his statement, "Gil, you are cruel," he should have said something like this: "Your behavior has hurt Marvin. I would be glad to help you make it up to him. How could you do that?" *Teachers are more likely to be successful with students who see the teacher as on their side.*

Lorraine's Story

Last week Candy told me that she was being hit in the back with spitballs. Students often bully Candy. Just last week someone zip-tied her backpack to her chair. The students were testing me, I had to deal with it, but I didn't know how.

I told the class that the spitballs must stop, that those throwing them were being rude and disruptive and preventing others from learning. I also told them that everyone would have to stay after class until I found out who was doing it.

At the end of the class, two boys approached me and admitted to having thrown the spitballs, but they said they were throwing them at each other, not at Candy. They also said that others were involved, but they didn't know who they were. Thanking them for coming forward, I let the rest of the class go. Then I told the boys that since they had known that throwing the spitballs would be wrong but they had done it anyway, I would have to write them up.

Still, I was troubled. They were the ones being punished, but those who hadn't come forward were getting away without a consequence. Second, I wasn't sure whether the boys had been aiming at Candy, a more serious offense than throwing the spitballs at each other.

I decided to speak with my assistant principal to see how I should have handled the situation. He said that a teacher should never punish the whole class, that writing up a student should be the last resort, and that the teacher should address a **discipline problem** herself before involving others. He also reassured me that every new teacher experiences such a problem and that you can't know the best way to handle it until you've faced it a few times.

(Continued)

(Continued)

When I saw the class again, I pulled the two boys aside and told them that, yes, their behavior was inappropriate and unacceptable, but I had overreacted and wasn't going to write them up. They were relieved, and I was somewhat satisfied. Still, I wonder how I should have handled the problem in the first place.

Lorraine learned two lessons from her assistant principal. First, *never impose group punishment.* It punishes the innocent while demonstrating your own inability to deal with a problem justly.

Second, writing up a student, presumably for an administrative intervention such as a detention, should be the last resort. In other words, *an administrative intervention should be reserved for an emergency*, such as for violence or the threat of violence, or after a teacher's own repeated but unsuccessful attempts to solve a problem (see Chapter 29 for other examples of occasions for an administrative intervention). After thinking it over, Lorraine rescinded her decision to write them up. Like Lorraine, *don't be afraid to admit your mistakes*.

Despite these lessons, Lorraine still didn't learn how to handle instances of students bullying Candy or throwing spitballs. How would you advise her?

How could you reduce the likelihood of bullying in your own classroom?

Note: Bullying Triangle

Sullivan, Cleary, and Sullivan (2004) introduce the concept of the bullying triangle consisting of the bully, the victim, and bystanders. Bystanders contribute to the abuse by supporting the bully. To change the dynamic, bystanders need to be taught to support the victim instead.

- Sullivan, K., Cleary, M., & Sullivan, G. (2004). *Bullying in secondary schools: What it looks like and how to manage it.* London: Chapman.

When Students Cheat

Two **novice teachers,** Angela and Elsie, each had reason to believe that a pair of students had cheated during a test, and each privately discussed her concerns with the students afterwards. Ultimately, each teacher could reasonably believe that her students would not share their answers with each other again. Yet Angela was frustrated with her outcome, whereas Elsie was pleased with hers. How did their approaches differ?

(Continued)

Barbara and Winnie sit next to each other. Barbara is a **good student,** whereas Winnie struggles with the material. During group work, Barbara tends to share her work with the others in her group, and I have had to remind her that the others must provide input as well.

The thought that they might have cheated crushed me. It felt like a personal affront, although I understand that their behavior has little to do with me. I decided I would confront them together in my office the next day, and if they had cheated, both girls would get a zero on the test.

When I met with them, I told them I had seen the same pattern of right and wrong answers on their papers and wanted to know what explanation they had for me. They denied cheating, but based on how they responded, I believe that Winnie copied from Barbara's paper but Barbara was unaware of it. Without proof, however, I didn't feel comfortable punishing Winnie. So I told them I accepted their statements and their grades would stand, but I would change their seats.

Overall, I was frustrated with the outcome. I was upset that they had cheated and that without proof, I could do nothing. But at least I didn't embarrass them.

Angela may have needed to make explicit the distinction between group work as a learning activity and testing as an assessment activity in order to explain to her students why they would have to work independently on their tests. *Students need to understand the rationale behind a rule, **routine,** or expectation, that each is not simply an arbitrary attempt to control their behavior.*

Moreover, Angela could better secure her short-answer test results by preparing two versions of the test, the versions differing in the order of the items, and administering each version in alternate rows. She would then have a **proactive management strategy** to replace the **reactive management strategy** of separating the students after she suspected them of having cheated. *Proactive management strategies are better than reactive management strategies.*

Elsie's Story

About 10 minutes into the test, I notice two students, good students, looking at each other's test papers. Roy leaned toward Lori, and at the same time, Lori moved her paper a little closer to Roy.

I saw red! I felt like yelling, getting out of my seat, and tearing their papers to shreds. But I didn't. I remembered how I had seen other teachers handle this situation. And I remembered being an insecure student myself and needing the validation I got when I saw that another student had answers the same as mine.

I waited until after class and asked the students to come into my office. Then I calmly said, "I didn't like what I saw during the test. I don't want to see it again." Instead of a stream of denials, they apologized and assured me that it would not happen again.

I was pleased with this conversation. I held the discussion in private to avoid embarrassing them, I conveyed the message that I would not tolerate their behavior, and they made a commitment to stop.

Despite their anger, Angela and Elsie each postponed the discussion with their students until they could address the situation calmly. *Teachers need to be the model of a rational, temperate, consistent, and positive adult, the only such model some of their students may ever see.* Then, without preaching, each briefly presented her concerns to the pair in private. *A private conversation preserves the student's or students' dignity, thereby forestalling a defensive or hostile response.*

Elsie's approach, however, was more effective than Angela's. Angela, presenting her students with an implicit accusation, focused on what they had done, namely, produce an identical pattern of answers, and what they should do, namely, provide her with an explanation. On the other hand, Elsie focused on her own feelings. She said, "I didn't like . . ." and "I don't want. . . ." *Instead of criticizing* [even implicitly] *the actions of their students, teachers can safely express their anger by referring to their own feelings.*

Angela expected to resolve the situation by eliciting an admission and imposing a penalty. On the other hand, Elsie, softened by memories of her own schooldays and informed by the strategies of other teachers, chose a "working with" rather than a "doing to" approach. *A "working with" rather than a "doing to" approach promotes student maturity.* Thus Angela, with no admission or any other proof to justify imposing a penalty, became frustrated, whereas Elsie, eliciting not only an admission but their commitment to stop, was pleased.

How do your values and beliefs about cheating compare with Angela's or Elsie's?

Note to Elsie's Story: Expressing Anger Safely

Ginott (1972) advises teachers to express their anger without insult and their indignation without indignity. When angry, teachers should describe what they see, how they feel, and what they expect. In other words, teachers should attack the problem, not the person. They should give an "I" message, not a "you" message.

- Ginott, H. G. (1972). *Teacher and child: A book for parents and teachers.* New York: Macmillan.

Similarly, Gordon (1989) uses the "I" message as a way for the teacher to alert students to the impact their disruptive behavior is having on others.

- Gordon, T. (1989). *Teaching children self-discipline at home and in school.* New York: Random House.

When Students Fight

Classrooms are crowded places, order is fragile, and violence or the threat of violence can erupt suddenly. In the following two **stories,** Barney and Arthur each learn that **novice teachers** need eyes in the back of their head.

Barney's Story

During my study hall, I was helping one of my language arts students with his homework. I was oblivious to the rest of the study hall as I talked with him about character, plot, setting, and theme. But then I heard a loud noise. One boy was grabbing another by the shirt and pushing him to the floor between a row of tables. With a million things running through my mind, I sat there horrified for what seemed like an eternity. I thought, "I can't break up this fight" and "What if the whole class jumps in? This is out of control." I even thought about which of the two boys I liked better. Why would I think of something like that? I was stunned and didn't know what to do.

After all these thoughts, I jumped up, puffed myself up like a blowfish, and charged toward them. I saw a stunning change in both

(Continued)

(Continued)

of them almost immediately. They changed from giant gladiators into wide-eyed, 15-year-old boys. Then I said in my deepest voice, "Let it slide."

The whole incident lasted only about half a second, but it seemed longer. They both sat down, and later in the period, they were laughing together once again.

Novice teachers have difficulty claiming their power as the authority. Nevertheless, Barney prepared himself to assume this unfamiliar role, charged toward the boys, and with a resolute stance and deep voice, issued a terse order. *Teachers can strengthen a signal with multiple cues.*

Fights can erupt in a study hall because some students cannot manage the unstructured time. *Unstructured time generates boredom, restlessness, and disruption.* Teachers who monitor study halls can reduce the likelihood of a fight by bringing along newspapers, magazines, puzzles, or collections of short stories. *Proactive management strategies are better than reactive management strategies.*

Although the boys quickly reconciled, Barney still needed to speak with them separately and privately about their behavior. *A private conversation preserves the student's or students' dignity, thereby forestalling a defensive or hostile response.* First, he needed to allow them to express their feelings, but then he needed to explain to them the difference between feelings and behavior, that someone can feel angry but never has the right to assault another person. *A teacher should be strict about students' behavior but permissive about their feelings.*

Second, he needed to explain to them how their aggressive behavior could cause them to lose status with their peers. Third, he needed to coach them to recognize when they are becoming angry and to verbalize rather than act on how they feel.

Arthur's Story

The incident that stands out in my mind is when a boy wrote his name with a marker on the back of a girl's brand-new sweatshirt. The students had been doing an activity to trace the sun's path across the sky. They had gone outside to record marks on a plastic hemisphere to represent the positions of the sun. Once inside, they had to use that marker to trace the sun's path on that hemisphere.

The students were working well in their assigned groups. As I was concentrating on helping one particular group, a girl in the back of the room suddenly screamed, "You asshole!" and started to go after a boy in a neighboring group. I stepped between them just as she was about to pin him in the corner. I asked her to wait for me in my office until I could get another teacher to watch the class.

She explained that she had been working with her group when, for no reason at all, the boy wrote his name on her back with the marker. Between sobs, she told me that her ruined sweatshirt had cost her $80.

When I reminded her that the markers were dry-erase so the writing would wash off, her mood changed instantly. Then I called the boy into my office, and with a big smile on her face, she playfully called him a jerk. He apologized, adding that he had known the writing would wash off. By the time they left the office, the incident was just a big joke.

I lucked out. Had the marker been permanent, I would have had to send him to the principal's office for deliberately provoking a fight and destroying her property. And I learned that teachers need eyes in the back of their head. Dangerous things can happen quickly, so even when their attention is focused on one thing, teachers still need to be aware of everything else that's going on.

Arthur wisely waited to speak with the girl until he could get another teacher to watch his class. *Never leave your class unattended.* In the meantime, he removed her from the conflict and gave her time to calm down.

Both Barney and Arthur would have benefited from having eyes in the back of their head. Novice teachers, however, are usually incapable of **overlapping,** that is, of attending to two or more situations or tasks simultaneously. For example, while tutoring one student or group, they are likely to over-look the threat of disorder elsewhere. As a result, Barney and Arthur were each oblivious to the budding conflict.

You too are likely to be oblivious to developing conflicts in your classroom. You can, however, be ready with a strategy for confronting the fight. First, order the students to stop. They may be so engrossed, however, that they don't hear you, but simultaneously flashing the lights or making a loud noise might help get their attention.

If they do not respond immediately, then call for or send a reliable student for help while you protect the safety of the others. *Your first priority is to protect the other students and your-self.* Order the other students to move out of the way, even to line up in the hall. The last thing you would want is for any of them to be injured or embroiled in a fray.

Then, to the extent that you can do so safely, move objects such as desks, chairs, equipment, and personal possessions out of the way. *Your second priority is to protect the students who are fighting. Your third priority is to protect property.* Later, when all is calm, you can speak separately and privately with the students who were fighting.

Note: Overlapping and Withitness

Whereas overlapping refers to teachers attending to two or more situations or tasks simultaneously, **withitness** refers to their communicating to their students that they know what their students are up to. With-it teachers are the ones students say have eyes in the back of their head. Kounin (1970) invented these two related concepts to measure teachers' classroom management ability, with overlapping a necessary skill to achieve withitness.

- Kounin, J. S. (1970). *Discipline and group management in classrooms*. New York: Holt, Rinehart & Winston.

Once she could overlap, that is, simultaneously monitor separate groups of students, Kerrie, Bullough's first-year teacher, could execute more elaborate and interesting lessons.

- Bullough, R. V., Jr. (1989). *First-year teacher: A case study*. New York: Teachers College Press.

Note: Adolescent Conflict Resolution

Jones and Jones (2001) developed a seven-step plan for solving classroom conflicts. According to the plan, the teacher asks the conflicting parties such questions as, What happened? Is this behavior helping you or others? How could you have behaved differently? And are you willing to commit to changing your behavior?

- Jones, V., & Jones, L. (2001). *Comprehensive classroom management: Creating communities of support and solving problems* (6th ed.). Boston: Allyn & Bacon.

When You Find Yourself in a Power Struggle

In the first set of **stories,** each of two **novice teachers** explains how to avoid a power struggle. In the second set, each of three novice teachers (one of them being Brett, whose story you first read in Chapter 2) becomes ensnared in a power struggle. Which recommendations from the first set did the teachers in the second set fail to heed?

AVOIDING A POWER STRUGGLE

Jack's Story

I have developed a way to communicate my expectations to students. I speak calmly and detail what I want. I have learned that when you want something done, you should use persuasion, not force. I use kind words and simple logic. They respond to reasoned requests, not commands.

Here's an example. Students leave their books out on the desks. I have found that if you tell a student, "Put that book away," the student will come up with an excuse, such as, "That book is not mine. I already put mine away." On the other hand, I can ask a student to put a book away even when I know it isn't his. "Ralph, would you mind putting that book away for me, please? . . . Thank you." Without fail, Ralph will put the book away, no excuses.

I understand that when you're frustrated, it is hard to maintain your composure, but I find it calming to speak to the students this way. Many are not used to this demonstration of respect, but they appreciate it. I get more cooperation when I remain calm and explain what is wrong and what we are going to do about it.

Jack practices four practical principles to avoid a power struggle. First, he expresses his wishes as a request rather than a demand. He knows that *issuing an order promotes defiance, not cooperation.* Second, rather than charging his requests with blame, he focuses on a solution. He knows to *address the situation, not the shortcomings of the student(s).*

Third, Jack justifies his requests. *Students need to understand the rationale behind a rule, **routine,** or expectation, that each is not simply an arbitrary attempt to control their behavior.* And last, he knows that *teachers cannot control their students' behaviors, although they can influence and react to them. Teachers can, however, control their own behavior.* Accordingly, he behaves calmly and respectfully.

Shari's Story

My Spanish class has only 12 students, so I assigned each one a different verb. Each student was to prepare a poster to depict the meaning of the verb and compose two sentences in Spanish, each with a correct present-tense form of the verb. Then, while standing in front of the class, the student would read the sentences while displaying the poster.

(Continued)

(Continued)

   One particularly shy student refused to read his sentences. So I quickly said, "Okay, Jeff. I'll read your sentences while you display your poster." He readily agreed, and the lesson proceeded smoothly.

   I was able to avoid a power struggle because I knew Jeff well enough to propose an alternative he would accept. Pushing students results only in their dragging their feet or digging in their heels. I have learned that if I get to know my students, I can offer a compromise that will avoid a power struggle.

Sensitive to their distress, Shari accommodates her students. She is on their side. *Teachers are more likely to be successful with students who see the teacher as on their side.*

Note to Shari's Story: Shy Students

Shari wisely forestalled the buildup of Jeff's resistance and anxiety. However, she needs to be careful that she doesn't support his shyness. Instead, she needs to pressure him steadily but patiently to change, beginning with his actively participating in small-group activities.

- Good, T. L., & Brophy, J. E. (2008). *Looking in classrooms* (10th ed.). Boston: Pearson.

BECOMING ENSNARED IN A POWER STRUGGLE

Brett's Story

Last week in my consumer math class, I was challenged to maintain classroom discipline. This class has 13 ninth and tenth graders, nearly all doing poorly and showing little respect for anyone in the room.

> The particular student who challenged me, Joe, had recently returned from a 5-day suspension. He has a well-developed physique and enjoys showing it off.
>
> I began the class by asking the students to study for the quiz I was going to give them later in the period. At first, Joe didn't want to study, so I threatened to give the quiz to the class right then and there. The other students, however, convinced him to take out his notebook and study. After about a minute, he began to talk to the student next to him, so I moved Joe's seat to the back of the room. After about another minute, he began talking to the same student again, now from across the room. At this point, I told him to stop talking and study for the quiz. To this he answered, "What are you gonna do if I don't?"
>
> I threatened him again, this time to write a referral on him. So he quickly quieted down because he had been told that if he got any more referrals, he could be thrown out of school.
>
> I felt I took the proper steps. I knew from his other teachers that Joe's father has him on a short leash. So after moving his seat, I knew that the next step, threatening him with a referral, would work.

Brett provoked the confrontation. Rather than approach Joe with a request or even an order, Brett issued a threat. *Using threats (or bribes) to control student behavior undermines any potential for a mutually respectful relationship.* Second, Brett rebuked Joe publicly instead of privately or at least discreetly. *A private conversation preserves the student's or students' dignity, thereby forestalling a defensive or hostile response.*

How should Brett have approached Joe? If Brett was angry with Joe for disrupting the class's study time, he could have expressed his anger by referring to his own feelings. For example, he could have said to Joe, again privately, "I am upset that this study time is being wasted. Everyone here needs to study." *Instead of criticizing the actions of their students, teachers can safely express their anger by referring to their own feelings.* Or he could have said, "You've been out a few days.

How can I help you settle in?" *A "working with" rather than a "doing to" approach promotes student maturity.*

Then, if Joe continued to resist, Brett could offer him a choice. "You have a choice: Stay and give everyone a chance to study or go to the Guidance Office for the rest of the period. I hope you'll stay, but the choice is yours." *Offering a choice fosters autonomy rather than dependency and lessens defiance.* Believing that he responded appropriately, however, and that Joe had provoked the confrontation, Brett is likely to perpetuate this cycle of antagonism with Joe. *Only when you recognize your own contribution to a problem do you have any power to solve it.* (See Brett's Story in Chapter 2 for an analysis of his lesson.)

Roger's Story

On Wednesday, our team of teachers and 112 students went on a field trip to a power plant. After lunching by the river, I noticed several pieces of trash on the tables and grass. I asked the students whether any of them had left the trash. Several of the boys closest to the trash answered, "No." Then I asked if any of the boys would help me clean up the area so the trash wouldn't blow into the river. "It's not ours," they answered.

As I was collecting the trash from a table, I asked Bobby to pick up the plastic bag at his feet. He picked it up, but then promptly threw it down. I ordered him to pick it back up as I saw it was about to blow into the river. He complied and together we walked to the trash can. Neither one of us was pleased with the other. When I told him we were all responsible for keeping the area clean and preventing the trash from blowing into the river, he shouted, "Shut up!" and started pumping his fists. I reported the incident to the other teachers and learned that last Saturday, he had punched the quarterback after the football game.

While my group was waiting to board our bus back to school, I heard a commotion and saw a teacher escorting another boy, pale and trembling, off one of the buses. Bobby had punched him in the head.

What did I learn from this event? Do not assume that a student will react as you intend him or her to react. I thought I could get Bobby to help me, but he saw my request as a demand.

Roger got no cooperation when he asked the boys to help him clean up, probably because of the way he asked. Given his preceding question, "Who left this trash?" volunteering to help would be a boy's implicit admission that the trash was his. Hoping to avoid taking the blame, the boys answered, "It's not ours." Instead, Roger should have asked for help at the outset, saying something like Jack said to Ralph: "Boys, would you mind helping me pick up this trash, please? . . . Thank you."

Still, Roger's mistake in framing his initial request would have been inconsequential had it not led first to his ordering Bobby to pick up the plastic bag and then to his stream of moral platitudes to justify his order. *Teach (by example); don't preach.* Platitudes patronize. Roger's platitudes triggered Bobby's outburst. Roger's biggest mistake, however, was that he singled out Bobby to help him when he really didn't know him.

Note to Roger's Story: Revenge-Seeking Students

Bobby is an example of a **revenge-seeking student,** a student who feels that he has no control over his environment and that others disregard him and treat him unfairly. Such students are likely to erupt with anger and abuse in response to any demand or reprimand. For interventions for revenge-seeking students, see the following:

- Charles, C. M. (2002). *Building classroom discipline* (7th ed.). Boston: Allyn & Bacon.
- Nelson, J. (1987). *Positive discipline*. New York: Ballantine.

Guadaloupe's Story

The first day we used microscopes in my seventh-grade class, I made a point of stating the rules. In particular, I emphasized the importance of always carrying a microscope with two hands. No sooner had I made the point—more than once in fact—than I saw a student carrying his with one hand. I called out, "Two hands, Lloyd," to remind him of the rule. Lloyd became surly and argumentative about the rule.

(Continued)

(Continued)

I don't argue with students, so I simply repeated the rule, expecting to end the incident. I had no intention of giving him a punishment since this was our first day using the microscopes. But he continued to argue with me, making excuses for using only one hand, saying that his desk was close to the shelf where the microscopes are stored. I asked him to stop arguing with me.

But he continued, this time muttering, "This is so stupid." So I gave him a lunch detention for being disrespectful.

"Well, I'm not going."

I ignored his comment, figuring he was just showboating and if I didn't give him any more attention, I could continue my class. When I gave him the lunch detention slip, however, he repeated that he wouldn't show up. I ignored his statement. In fact, I was probably more lenient with him than other teachers would have been.

When he didn't go to lunch detention, I had to refer him to the assistant principal for insubordination. There I learned that he has been slipping academically and socially and is in the same sort of trouble with his other teachers.

The assistant principal had him apologize, but the apology, hardly sincere, was certainly no solution to Lloyd's **misbehavior.** I am not satisfied with the outcome even though I followed the school's procedure for such a situation.

Guadaloupe issued Lloyd a succinct, albeit public reminder to use two hands. It was hardly an order. Given the threat to classroom safety, her immediate and direct intervention was appropriate, even necessary. She should not, however, have issued him a detention for muttering. On the contrary, a teacher should *ignore behaviors that hardly interfere with teaching or learning.* Besides, *punishment does not deter misbehavior; it fosters resentment, not cooperation.* And his defiance was waning anyway.

If Guadaloupe had been determined to issue him a detention, then she should have taken the time to do it privately. Moreover, she should have explained why. She could have said, "I see we're not in sync right now. Come in at lunchtime and let's see if we can work it out." With only a broadcasted order for him to report to detention, he predictably rebelled.

Guadaloupe was dissatisfied with the outcome. She knew she had lost ground in her relationship with Lloyd. Her approach had been to "do to" rather than "work with" him. Inasmuch as Lloyd's problems in school had become chronic, the most promising strategy for working with him would have been to foster a trusting rather than authoritarian relationship with him. *The development of a trusting relationship with a caring adult is the most effective strategy for treating a student with a chronic school problem.* Such a relationship, however, can take considerable time to foster, not necessarily a realistic expectation for a novice teacher. Nevertheless, what first step should Guadaloupe have taken to avoid a power struggle with Lloyd?

When Your Student Has a Tantrum

I n this chapter, three **novice teachers** each demonstrate how to turn a student's tantrum into an opportunity to foster cooperation. They upheld their standard of behavior with kindness rather than punishment. The fourth **story** is about a teacher who also thought he was successful. Still, you might have ideas about what he could have done differently.

Rebecca's Story

On the day before a unit test, I was reviewing the material with the class, and Chris came in announcing that he was going to fail. By talking to the other students, yelling out obviously wrong answers, and getting out of his seat, he made focusing the class on the review impossible. I stopped the oral review and instead had the students read a summary of the material to themselves.

While they were reading, I pulled up a chair and sat down next to Chris, saying, "I don't think you're giving yourself enough credit. I have seen the work you produce when you think you can do it and when you focus yourself. I have faith in you, and I know that if you really pay attention during this review and go over the notes a few times tonight, you will do just fine. Do you think you can do this?"

He looked at me and said, "Okay," but his eyes said more. He looked so relieved and grateful. During the rest of the class, I continued with the oral review. Chris was cooperative, raising his hand to volunteer correct information, and was a great example for the rest of the class.

I think Chris just needed to know that I cared, that I understood his fear, and that I believed in him. I have found that many disruptions are caused by students who are afraid of failure or embarrassed because they do not understand the material.

Rebecca's immediate restructuring of the learning activity disengaged Chris from his audience and enabled her to converse with him privately. *A private conversation preserves the student's or students' dignity, thereby forestalling a defensive or hostile response.* Then, rather than scold or preach, she dealt with his distress. She acknowledged his fears, suggested a strategy to direct his efforts, expressed confidence in him, and elicited his commitment to study. *Communicating high expectations is likely to improve student behavior as well as achievement.*

Ariana's Story

One particular incident happened during my middle school study hall. In the beginning of the year, I had difficulty conducting a study hall because some students wanted to talk, even rather loudly, and some wanted to do their work. Therefore, during our second session, the students and I together came up with a rule. They could speak to each other but only quietly so that others could do their work.

(Continued)

(Continued)

During the second week, Linda came to class late. She entered noisily and would not sit down. First, I said hello to her and asked her to please sit down. Since she had been in this study hall from the beginning, she was familiar with our rules. She refused to sit in a chair, sitting on a desk instead and talking loudly with another student. I asked her again to sit down, and she told me to f— off. I then very calmly told her to step outside the classroom.

I allowed Linda to stand outside the classroom for a minute so she could cool down and I could collect my thoughts. When I asked her what her problem was, she answered that I should not tell her what to do. I explained that she herself had helped to set up the rule. I then continued to explain that I should not and would not tolerate that kind of language in the classroom or anywhere else for that matter. I told her that if she was really against the rule, I would help her transfer to another study hall. Then I waited a while and said that most people have a bad day now and then but that taking it out on others doesn't solve anything. I waited again and then asked her what she planned to do. She said that she would remain in the study hall and that she would come back in and try to follow the rule. I agreed and decided not to write her up for inappropriate language.

The following day Linda came into the classroom a different person. The first thing she did was apologize to me for what she had said the previous day. I accepted her apology, thanked her, and since that day, I haven't had a problem with Linda.

Ariana's response was similar to Rebecca's. In acknowledging Linda's bad day, Ariana accepted her student's feelings but upheld her standard of behavior. *A teacher should be strict about students' behavior but permissive about their feelings.* Ariana also spoke privately with her student, keeping her message brief and focused on a solution.

First, Ariana reminded Linda that Linda herself had participated in creating the rule. *If students have made a commitment to a rule, especially one they had a share in creating, they are likely to correct their **misbehavior** with simply a reminder of the rule.* Second, Ariana gave Linda a choice about staying in the study hall.

Offering a choice fosters autonomy rather than dependency and lessens defiance. Third, Ariana gave them both a chance to calm down, and she gave Linda the time to make a thoughtful decision.

Last, like Rebecca, Ariana elicited her student's commitment to cooperate, in this case to follow the rule.

Mary's Story

All my eighth-grade classes are rambunctious, but my first-period class is both rambunctious and insolent. The day was a testing day, when the first 2 hours would be for the students to take a standardized test with their first-period teacher. The time needed, however, is only about an hour and 15 minutes.

Debby has been a defiant student. She entered the room totally unprepared, as usual. The students had been told to bring two pencils and their novels from English class to read after they finished the test. I asked Debby where her pencils and book were and escorted her to her locker where I was rewarded with a string of colorful expletives and told to get out of her face and mind my own business. I chose to disregard the verbal assault and calmly said that her education was my business and I knew she could behave if she put her mind to it. She acknowledged my statement with another verbal assault.

A patient and saintly veteran teacher witnessing the event kindly asked whether Debby could take the test in her room. Debby was directed across the hall to the teacher's **time-out** table, and I brought her the test booklet. I told her that no matter how she felt about me, she had a lot of potential, and this test would decide which classes she would take next year. I told her that her future was her responsibility, no one else's, and the choice was hers. Then I left the room.

I handled it that way because I didn't know what else to do. Honestly, I was in shock. But I learned that maintaining control and sending a student to another teacher could be the best things to do. I later received a nice note from Debby followed by a face-to-face apology. She explained that she had had a particularly bad weekend at home and exploded at the first authority figure she encountered. Also, she told the other teacher that my comment to her before the test was the first time anyone had told her that she had potential.

(Continued)

(Continued)

I am learning that each incident has a history and must be handled in an individual way. Debby is still a handful, but I have seen a big improvement. The frequency of her outbursts has diminished, and she has pulled her grade up from an F to a C+. I continue to encourage her while holding her accountable, and she seems to be receptive.

Like the other teachers, Mary turned her student's tantrum into an opportunity to foster cooperation. She discussed Debby's behavior with her in private, expressed confidence in her, offered her a choice, refrained from preaching, and, instead, focused on a solution. And, like the others, while acknowledging her student's feelings, Mary upheld her standard of behavior.

Also like the others, Mary worked with Debby as an advocate, not as an adversary. *Teachers are more likely to be successful with students who see the teacher as on their side.* Accordingly, Debby cooperated in response not to bribes or threats but to an understanding of her own responsibility for her future and the importance of the test. Last, Mary took advantage of the veteran teacher's offer of a time-out, an opportunity for Debby to calm down, comparable to the time Ariana gave Linda.

None of the novice teachers seemed to take the tantrum personally. To minimize frustration and maintain your equilibrium, *resist the tendency to take your students' misbehaviors personally.* Chris, Linda, and Debby each exploded in response to a personal problem, not to anything their teacher had done. Last, all three novice teachers used kindness rather than punishment to discipline their student. *Punishment does not deter misbehavior; it fosters resentment, not cooperation.* And *good discipline is achieved through a series of small kindnesses,* sometimes over many weeks, if not months.

Note to Ariana's and Mary's Stories: Time-Out

Kohn (2006a) makes the distinction between a time-out that the teacher offers and one the teacher imposes. The former, the only one he recommends, is an option the student can elect in order to gain composure in a safe place. The latter, he claims, is a punishment that isolates and humiliates the student without solving the problem.

- Kohn, A. (2006a). *Beyond discipline: From compliance to community, 10th anniversary edition.* Alexandria, VA: Association for Supervision and Curriculum Development.

Now consider Theodore's response to a student who asked for permission to leave the classroom.

Theodore's Story

The opportunity to confront my first behavior problem arose with a girl in my algebra class. I knew from previous interactions with her that she had an opposition personality. The rule was that no one could leave the room when the class was in session. They could leave only before or after class or during the break.

During this particular class, she asked to go to the bathroom. When her request was denied, she sat back down in her chair and began voicing her displeasure. As I continued to teach the class, she got up from her seat and quietly walked in front of the class and out the door, probably to the bathroom. I continued with the lesson.

Several minutes later, she returned to her seat. I did not make a scene, but later that day, I wrote a referral for her insubordination. I assume she met with an administrator and the appropriate actions were taken. My colleagues agreed that I acted correctly. I was not drawn into a confrontation with her, and I kept her from distracting the class further. Since that time, she has not spoken to me about the referral, but she has not misbehaved either.

How else could Theodore have managed the situation?

27

When a Student Persistently Seeks Attention

In the first five of these **stories,** the **novice teachers** explain how they each dealt with a student who persistently seeks attention. In the last story, the teacher asks for advice in dealing with such a student.

Claire's Story

I have a student who is 19 and in the 13th grade. His name is Devon. He constantly seeks attention in one of two ways: telling others to be quiet and pay attention or disrupting the class by talking, joking, or even getting up and walking around (ostensibly to blow his nose or sharpen a pencil). He never turns in an assignment.

One day, Devon was leaning back, his chair inclined, his feet on his desk. His shirt was pulled halfway up, revealing a belly-button ring. He was pulling a string through the ring, back and forth. The rest of the class was on task, relatively speaking, and we were on a roll. Rather than speak to Devon, I ignored him for a while. Then, as

I walked by him—I circulate around the room continuously—I gave him a look of disgust. He laughed. I did not. Surprisingly, a few others snickered.

Devon sat up and stopped his string-through-the-ring trick. I was not only surprised that his classmates snickered at his behavior but amazed that he cared how I or his classmates reacted.

Instead of publicly ordering him to stop his string-through-the-ring trick, Claire gave Devon an opportunity first to control his own behavior. *Rather than impose control, a teacher should foster students' self-control.* Her initial strategy was **planned ignoring.** That is, she noticed his behavior but intentionally and completely ignored it. A teacher should *ignore behaviors that hardly interfere with teaching or learning.* Because Devon was not disturbing the rest of the class, Claire could wait to see whether he would stop by himself.

Then, when his behavior persisted, she followed up with a subtle but direct intervention, approaching his desk and looking at him disapprovingly. *Nonverbal signals are better than verbal signals because they do not provoke defensive arguments or hostile confrontations. Nonverbal signals also do not interrupt the flow of the lesson, and they invite the students to control their own behavior.* Whether Devon stopped in response to her look of disgust or his classmates' derision, he came to control his own behavior.

Claire moved toward a direct intervention only when necessary. *Teachers need a systematic management plan ranging from subtle to progressively more direct and intrusive interventions.* Had Devon's behavior continued, Claire would have had to intervene more intrusively. For example, if the other students were working on a set of problems, she could have stopped at his desk and said, "Let's see how you're doing with these problems." If she was lecturing, she could have tapped on his desk as she circulated about the room or called on him with a straightforward question. If Devon persisted further, then she would have had to speak with him privately as the novice teachers in each of the next three stories did.

Note to Claire's Story: Planned Ignoring

Planned ignoring is often ineffective because even if the teacher ignores the **misbehavior,** students may encourage it. Therefore, it should be attempted only when the misbehavior is minor, such as when a student daydreams or calls out an answer.

- Brophy, J. E. (1988). Educating teachers about managing classrooms and students. *Teaching and Teacher Education, 4,* 1–18.
- Levin, J., & Nolan, J. F. (2007). *Principles of classroom management: A professional decision-making model* (5th ed.). Boston: Allyn & Bacon.

Gary's Story

Mike has a history of interrupting our lessons with his talking and fooling around. I have heard more than one teacher say that he is 15 going on 11. On this particular day, I had already spoken to him about his behavior at least three times. I stressed his need to stay on task and bring up his grades. Nevertheless, he continued to disrupt the class.

Earlier in the week, he and a few of the others had begun to play a game. Every so often during class, one of them would announce a celebrity's name, a name completely unrelated to our topic. The result was the laughter of a few and the distraction of many. I had announced that I would not tolerate this behavior, but today, it began again.

I was angry that these few would continue to disrupt in the very way I had told them not to, but I was trying hard to control myself. Then, in my frustration, I did something I'd never done before. I said, "The next person to blurt out something unrelated to the lesson will be sent to the principal's office."

After my announcement, about 2 minutes went by before Mike muttered, "Christian Slater." The name prompted a few chuckles and my swift action. I told Mike to leave. He had a hint of the "Who me?" expression on his face, but he left without an argument, and the lesson continued without further disruption.

In retrospect, I realize that once I voiced the consequence, I had to send him to the office. But I really don't like to do that sort of thing. Mike and I talked before class the next day. He apologized, and we discussed our different roles in the classroom. Will he still cause disruptions? Probably, but now that we have a relationship, he may cause fewer of them.

Gary hesitated to express his anger because he didn't know how to do it safely. *Instead of criticizing the actions of their students, teachers can safely express their anger by referring to their own feelings.* So instead of rebuking Mike and the others, he could, for example, have said, "I am upset because these outbursts are distracting from our lesson. We all deserve an opportunity to learn." Like most novices struggling to find an appropriate response, however, Gary said nothing at first and then shifted to the opposite extreme, issuing a threat. *Using threats (or bribes) to control student behavior* was not only useless but *undermines any potential for a mutually respectful relationship.*

The next day, Gary spoke privately with Mike. *A private conversation preserves the student's or students' dignity, thereby forestalling a defensive or hostile response.* By discussing their different roles, they could each come to understand each other's perspective. *A teacher needs to make sure that students understand the problem from the teacher's perspective and that he or she understands it from theirs.* As a result of Gary's approach, he and Mike began to build a relationship. *The development of a trusting relationship with a caring adult is the most effective strategy for treating a student with a chronic school problem.*

Clark's Story

Anthony is a disruptive student in my 10th-grade class. He is also the school's football hero. He constantly comes to class late and behaves disrespectfully. For example, he has gotten up in the middle of class, walked around, and at times, even sung aloud. To make matters worse, he is the ringleader in a class that, as a whole, has behavior problems and learning difficulties. During the first few weeks, I tried everything to get him under control, but he met my threats of detention, referrals, and suspension with his typical nonchalance.

So I had to try another strategy. I convinced him to stay after school for a few minutes so I could go over with him some of his work and get him caught up. I used this opportunity to speak with him more personally and informally. I first explained that his behavior reflected badly on me as a teacher. I also told him that I was not going to give up on him and that I was available every day for extra help or just to talk. Last, I explained to him that his behavior influences all the others and that I wanted him to be a positive example for the rest of the class. So far, the talk has worked, and I have let him know that I have noticed and appreciate his improvement.

By speaking with him as I would to an adult, I gave him the attention he needs and earned the opportunity to build a relationship with him. And now that he feels some responsibility for the progress of the class, he doesn't want to let me down.

Clark's strategies with Anthony, like Gary's with Mike, shifted from issuing threats to developing a trusting relationship. Clark's threats were based on two misconceptions prevalent among novice teachers, namely, that a teacher can control a student's behavior and that punishment deters misbehavior. On the contrary, *teachers cannot control their students' behaviors, although they can influence and react to them.* And second, *punishment does not deter misbehavior; it fosters resentment, not cooperation.* Clark was successful with Anthony only when he shifted from a "doing to" to a "working with" approach. *A "working with" rather than a "doing to" approach promotes student maturity.*

Scott's Story

Gloria is an energetic girl. Sometimes she contributes appropriately to the class discussion. More often, though, she vies for attention inappropriately. Early in a lesson, she raises her hand and waits to be called on, but when I don't call on her often enough, she gets restless.

One day, within the first few minutes of class, Gloria began shouting uncontrollably. Some outbursts were related to the lesson; others pertained to the color of my shirt or her feelings about the New York Yankees. At first, I acknowledged her comments and responded politely with the hope that the lesson could continue. Then, as her outbursts became more frequent, I asked her to raise her hand. But she only got worse.

So I decided to have a conversation with her. The next day, she came to class early, about 2 minutes before the bell. When I asked her to come up and speak with me for a moment, she approached eagerly. "Gloria, you are a **good student**," I said, "and you bring lots of energy to the class. That's why I need your help."

She peered at me, her head cocked to one side.

"I need you to raise your hand when you have something to say. Plus I would really appreciate it if you could help me and the rest of the class keep to the topic. Can you do that for me?"

"Sure. No problem."

And with that, the class began and went smoothly. She contributed to the discussion by raising her hand and offering insightful comments and thoughtful questions.

Like Gary with Mike and Clark with Anthony, Scott had a private conversation with Gloria, one in which she made a commitment to control herself. How long could Scott expect her to abide by her commitment? Not long, but should her outbursts continue, he can now remind her of her commitment with a simple signal, such as staring at her and shaking his head. *If students have made a commitment to a rule, especially one they had a share in creating, they are likely to correct their misbehavior with simply a reminder of the rule.* Moreover, Scott can commend her from time to time as her self-control improves.

Scott could also use a **proactive management strategy.** He can reduce the time the class spends on whole-class learning activities, such as lectures and **recitations,** and increase the time spent in small groups. *Whenever you have some students monopolizing the class's time, you need to decentralize instruction.* Gloria would be less likely to disrupt in a small group, and if she did, her impact would be restricted to that smaller audience.

Dawn's Story

I first moved Guy to the front of the room so he could focus on the lesson. However, this change was a mistake. He started to distract the others by muttering, calling out, making faces, and goofing off. He was in his glory while I had to compete with him for the class's attention.

Then I remembered stories about boys in school, the stories we've all heard, how some boys demand so much attention that the other students, especially the girls, are ignored. "Oh, no," I thought. "I have fallen into the trap!" So after a few days of his distractions, I calmly and sweetly told him that he would be sitting in another seat, this time in the very back of the classroom, beyond the last row.

This second seat change has worked. Guy no longer has an audience, and while I sometimes feel sorry for him—for only a fleeting moment—I realize that a seating arrangement affects the way a student behaves.

Dawn concentrated on only half the problem, stabilizing the learning environment. After Guy's first seat change, she did not consider any other strategies to help him focus on the lesson. As is characteristic of a novice teacher, she was concerned more with her teaching than her students' learning. How could Dawn have worked with Guy so as to integrate him into whole-class learning activities?

Abby's Story

Ivan monopolizes the class's time to tell me whether or not he's done his homework. He does poorly in school and relies on his homework to pass his courses. I have told him that doing the class work is just as (if not more) important as doing the homework. Nevertheless, he continues to ask about his homework even after I have calmly explained the importance of his concentrating on the task at hand.

When he persisted one day in following me around and asking me about his homework, I got angry, raised my voice, and threatened to send him to the office. I know this was not the right thing to do, but I don't know how to make him realize the importance of attending to his class work.

Abby's problem is somewhat different from the others. Ivan does not disrupt the class directly. Instead, he seeks attention from her alone, distracting her and wasting his own time. How can Abby help both Ivan and herself?

When a Student Provokes the Class's Animosity

George, a **novice teacher,** helped an unwitting boy understand how he was provoking the class's animosity. Instead of focusing on how to stop Moe's obnoxious remarks, George devised a way for Moe to become aware of the behavior himself.

George's Story

Moe, a student in my eighth-period class, is socially awkward, not cruel, his obnoxious remarks more a misfire than an aimed insult. The other students, already threatening to take matters into their own hands, have been demanding his transfer.

For several weeks, I tried to make Moe aware of his tactlessness, first through hints but then more directly. I also discussed Moe's behavior with several of his other teachers, past and present. Although they were aware of his problem, they could give me no advice other than to keep reminding him to keep his comments to himself.

I had recently begun to audiotape my sixth-period lessons to identify the conditions that trigger the chatter in that class. As I was listening to the tape, I realized that audiotaping might be just the method I could use with Moe. If he could hear himself making those clumsy remarks, then perhaps he could see how to stop them. So over the next 2 days, I also taped my eighth-period lessons.

As I replayed these tapes, I heard Moe making gratuitous remarks on at least six occasions. So on the third day, assuring him that he was not in any kind of trouble, I asked him to meet me after school.

When I played portions of the tapes for him, his eyes widened in disbelief. "Did I really say that? What could have prompted me to say such a thing?" I didn't answer. Rather, I gave him an opportunity to reflect. I did, however, assure him that people can change their behavior and that I was sure his words did not mirror his heart. Since that day, Moe has chosen his words carefully, and although he occasionally speaks without thinking, an apology is sure to follow.

George sought a more productive strategy than his veteran colleagues' recommendation. He sought to "work with" rather than "do to" Moe. *A "working with" rather than a "doing to" approach promotes student maturity.* In the privacy of an afterschool meeting, George helped Moe recognize the remarks that were alienating his classmates. *Students need specific and immediate feedback to recognize their behavior.* Once Moe recognized his contribution to the problem, he had the power to solve it. *Only when you recognize your own contribution to a problem do you have any power to solve it.*

George described Moe as socially awkward, not cruel, a perspective that predisposed him to guide rather than blame or punish Moe. As a result, Moe could see that George was on his side. *Teachers are more likely to be successful with students who see the teacher as on their side.* And last, George assured Moe that he could change. *The promise of redemption is a strong motivator.*

George fostered Moe's social development. How could you foster the social development of one of your students?

Note: Social Skills Training

Students like Moe are often unaware of how their behavior undermines their social acceptance and how they can behave otherwise. In most cases, they benefit from social skills training.

- Coie, J., Underwood, M., & Lochman, J. (1991). Programmatic intervention with aggressive children in the school setting. In D. Pepler & K. Rubin (Eds.), *The development and treatment of childhood aggression* (pp. 389–410). Hillsdale, NJ: Erlbaum.
- Furlong, M., & Smith, D. (Eds.). (1994). *Anger, hostility, and aggression: Assessment, prevention, and intervention strategies for youth.* Brandon, VT: Clinical Psychology Publishing.

29

When an Administrative Intervention Is Necessary

The first **story** is about Marilyn, who, as one of several chaperones, had to decide whether an administrative intervention was necessary. The second story is about Sari, who, rather than call for an administrative intervention, sought her administrator's advice instead.

Marilyn's Story

Four other teachers and I chaperoned two senior classes on a field trip. Dressed in jeans and carrying a backpack, I suppose I resembled a student myself. Some students knew who I was; others did not. No one bothered to ask.

(Continued)

(Continued)

While hiking, I overheard two boys discussing their plans to smoke marijuana. I watched as they patted their pockets with assurance.

Having witnessed their discussion, I knew I had to assert myself. I informed the teacher in charge, who then informed the other three chaperones. The teacher in charge then lagged behind to watch the boys for suspicious behavior. Soon after that, she confiscated a joint from the boy who was about to put it in his mouth.

This experience has enhanced my confidence as a leader and **novice teacher.** I knew what the right thing to do should be, and I did it. The next day, the assistant principal called me down to her office to commend my action, especially in light of my inexperience. Sadly, I know this situation could be the first of many.

Marilyn had the courage to exercise her authority but also the sense to realize its limitations. *An administrative intervention should be reserved for an emergency*, but what constitutes an emergency? The following are examples of a situation that would require an administrative intervention: violence or the threat of violence to a person or property; criminal activity such as stealing or the possession of drugs, alcohol, or a weapon; a student refusing to leave the room when the teacher orders it; or a trespasser on school property. Other grounds for the intervention of either an administrator or other school personnel, such as the school nurse, social worker, guidance counselor, or psychologist, would include evidence of truancy, a threat to the health of a student or the school community, possible child abuse, and extreme behaviors such as disrobing or self-mutilation.

Unlike administrative interventions, however, which should be reserved for emergencies, a conversation with an administrator, as Sari learned, can be an opportunity to gain insight.

Sari's Story

I was new to the school and to the experience of keeping a student for detention. What should I do with her for 45 minutes? I had assigned Fran to an afterschool detention for sticking a wad of bubble gum under her desk. Having failed to enforce the policy against chewing gum, I was now stuck with not just her wad, which was still gooey, but, as I came to see, a million others fossilized under the other desks.

As I was rushing out for bus duty, I passed the assistant principal and asked him what I should do with her during the detention. I shall never forget his answer. "It doesn't matter what you do with her," he said, "as long as your relationship with her is stronger when she leaves."

Fran and I worked side by side to clean up the desks, but more important, we talked. As a seventh grader, she, like me, was new to the school. So we each had a chance to compare this school with our former school. And I don't think she ever disposed of her gum like that again, at least not in my class.

Remember, save administrative interventions for emergencies like Marilyn's, but don't overlook opportunities for an administrator's advice.

Note: Crimes or Misbehaviors

Violence or the threat of violence, vandalism, theft, and the possession of drugs, alcohol, or weapons are crimes. Therefore, teachers need to refer these occurrences to the administration. On the other hand, classroom disruptions are **misbehaviors.** Thus teachers themselves are responsible for treating them.

- Levin, J., & Nolan, J. F. (2007). *Principles of classroom management: A professional decision-making model* (5th ed.). Boston: Allyn & Bacon.

Conclusion

Becoming an Effective Classroom Manager

All of a teacher's values, knowledge, and skills impact on **classroom management.** Becoming an effective **classroom manager** is, therefore, a developmental process. For example, as you learn about the curriculum, the instructional materials you have available, and your students, you will create lessons that appeal to their interests, relate to their experiences, and suit their abilities. And as you refine and expand that repertoire of lessons, you will build coherent instructional units and be able to make explicit the connections among the various lessons so your students can make sense of the curriculum. And as you gain confidence in your lessons, you will plan less for control and more for student learning, focusing more on your students' progress than your own performance. Your classroom management will improve with each of these gains. What's more, you will relax, and in doing just that, your classroom management will improve even more.

So how will you know when you're becoming an effective classroom manager? One clue is in Derek's Story:

Derek's Story

A boy in my second-period class is particularly troublesome. Mort does not participate in any activities and frequently disrupts the class. For example, he talks to the students around him, throws small objects, and gets out of his seat often. His behavior is a desperate gambit for attention, one I have yet to manage while teaching the rest of the class.

Mort has a long history of low achievement and borderline IQ scores. When I contact his parents, I get nowhere. Mort does no homework or class work and merely guesses on multiple-choice tests. He is failing the class with a solid 21% average.

When Mort once again proceeded to disrupt the class, I placed him in a neighboring teacher's classroom, gave him an assignment, and told him I would collect his work at the end of the period. Despite a few incorrect answers, he completed the assignment and behaved himself, and aside from my having to take the few minutes to get him settled next door, my own class went smoothly.

The strategy appears to have been effective, at least for the short term. But how can I address this problem for the long term?

- Having had some success with Mort in the short term, Derek looked for a long-term solution. Effective managers focus on strategies for long-term solutions. *Strategies for the short term may be necessary, but they are rarely sufficient.*

- Effective managers use **reactive management strategies** whenever necessary but **proactive management strategies** whenever possible. In Chapter 8, compare Adrienne's reactive strategy with Tiffany's proactive strategy. And in Chapter 18, compare the reactive strategy Tina used initially with the proactive strategy she used later. *Proactive management strategies are better than reactive management strategies.*

- Effective managers concentrate more on lesson execution than on discipline, more on maintaining student engagement than on treating **misbehavior.** For example, in Chapter 7, both Jenny and Jonathan struggled with a persistently noisy class. Jonathan negotiated with the entire class to accept a management plan that would advance his lessons. On the other hand, Jenny singled out Paul for a reprimand, thereby derailing her lesson.

Novice teachers can better concentrate on lesson execution when they have an appealing lesson with clear directions. *An appealing lesson is necessary but not sufficient to preclude most discipline problems.* Ryan and Jill (Chapter 1) each had such a lesson. On the other hand, Melissa, Charlotte, and Tara (Chapter 4) each had a promising lesson, but their students could not follow the directions and, in their frustration, generated disorder, even chaos.

Moreover, novice teachers can better concentrate on lesson execution when they use **routines** to structure regular classroom events. Routines streamline your teaching. *If used consistently, a routine minimizes the time and energy needed to direct a regular classroom event.* You don't have to belabor directions, and your students know what you expect of them. In Chapter 2, Michelle taught her students a routine for playing *Jeopardy!* In Chapter 6, Anne, Mark, and Jodi each established a routine for starting their lessons. And in Chapter 10, David reestablished a routine for his students to take daily note of their homework assignment.

- Effective managers anticipate problems and devise ways to circumvent them as they plan. *A teacher needs to consider both management and curricular objectives when planning and executing a lesson.* For example, Ira (Chapter 1), when planning to administer a test during the first half of a double period, decided to permit his students to take their customary break but only upon handing in their test paper. Similarly, Larry (Chapter 18) assigned each of his two most troublesome students to a high-status but demanding task in order to forestall their disrupting his lesson.

- Effective managers enforce their rules with consistency and ease because they have perfected a teaching role that suits their personality, students, and institutional culture. Novice teachers are still searching for that role. Like Mario (Chapter 17), Ollie (Chapter 22), and Gary (Chapter 27), they may vacillate between being too permissive and too harsh. Or like Jedd and Connor (Chapter 16), who each acted like a buddy to some of their students, they may assume a counterproductive role. Some, like Brett (Chapters 2 and 25), become a dictator, whereas others, like Leah (Chapter 7) and Connor (Chapter 16), reject that role.

- Effective managers overplan to prevent **dead time.** *Dead time generates disorder.* For example, to prevent dead time in the middle of her lesson, Lisa (Chapter 5) embedded enrichment tasks within her individual and group activities to occupy those who would otherwise finish ahead of their classmates. Luz (also Chapter 5) developed a supplementary activity for lesson closure, one she could append to any lesson to prevent dead time at the end.

- Effective managers execute brisk, activity-based lessons, ones with hardly an opportunity for misbehavior. Like Henry (Chapter 1), they anticipate the logistical hurdles and prepare their directions and organize their materials accordingly. On the other hand, Jason (also Chapter 1) came to realize how much preparation and organization are necessary to execute a brisk, activity-based lesson. *Preparation and organization are crucial to the execution of an activity-based lesson.*

- Effective managers **overlap;** that is, they attend to more than one situation or task simultaneously. For example, they respond to an inattentive student while delivering a lecture, or they monitor the rest of the class while tutoring one student or group. Many novice teachers are not yet able to overlap. Consequently, like Barney or Arthur (Chapter 24), they might not notice a conflict budding in their classroom.

- Effective managers reflect constructively on their actions, analyze essential aspects, and devise and try out alternatives to improve their lessons. For example, Amy (Chapter 9) reflected on Friday's chaos and revised her dissection lab for the classes scheduled to begin the activity on Monday.

When you practice many of these strategies all the time and all of these strategies some of the time, then you have become an effective classroom manager. Most of the student teachers practiced some of the strategies some of the time.

Given that order is fragile and classroom events occur swiftly and often unpredictably, however, no one, not even a seasoned teacher, can perform all the strategies all the time. For example, here is the **story** of Gail, an effective manager and 10-year veteran at the time of her story:

Gail's Story

I call my last-period students my reluctant learners, just to myself, of course. Some, however, are more than that. They are the school troublemakers. Last Wednesday, just as I was about to start my lesson, the assistant principal poked his head into my room to check on whether Cal was present.

"Yes, he's here, Mr. O'Leary."

Mr. O'Leary then asked me to hold Cal after class. He'd been trying to nail Cal to serve a string of afterschool detentions, but Cal had managed to slip away each time.

"Yes, I'll hold him."

"You won't forget now?"

"No, Mr. O'Leary. I promise."

As I said, the class is a challenge. As dismissal time approached, I performed my usual routines, inspecting the floor to see that the trash had been picked up and that the chairs were perched on the tabletops for the custodian. The kids were lined up by the door in anticipation of my signal, and then, with my wave and nod, they were gone, all of them, including Cal.

I had completely forgotten my promise to Mr. O'Leary until he once again poked his head into my room, this time to collect Cal.

"Oh, no! I can't believe it! I forgot to hold Cal. I am so sorry, so very sorry, Mr. O'Leary."

To my relief, he said, "That's all right, Gail. If Cal never does anything wrong again, he didn't need the detention. And if he does, I'll have another chance to get him."

Given the challenges of this particular class, Gail could not overlap sufficiently to attend to Cal while executing her dismissal routines. She did, however, learn a valuable lesson from Mr. O'Leary that day, that *there's always a tomorrow*, and in the meantime, she can *leave the problem at school.*

References

Brophy, J. E. (1988). Educating teachers about managing classrooms and students. *Teaching and Teacher Education, 4,* 1–18.

Bullough, R. V., Jr. (1989). *First-year teacher: A case study.* New York: Teachers College Press.

Canter, L., & Canter, M. (2001). *Assertive discipline: Positive behavior management for today's classrooms* (Rev. ed.). Los Angeles: Canter Associates.

Charles, C. M. (2002). *Building classroom discipline* (7th ed.). Boston: Allyn & Bacon.

Clarizio, H. F. (1980). *Toward positive classroom discipline* (3rd ed.). New York: Wiley.

Coie, J., Underwood, M., & Lochman, J. (1991). Programmatic intervention with aggressive children in the school setting. In D. Pepler & K. Rubin (Eds.), *The development and treatment of childhood aggression* (pp. 389–410). Hillsdale, NJ: Erlbaum.

Dillon, J. T. (1988). *Questioning and teaching: A manual of practice.* New York: Teachers College Press.

Dreikurs, R., & Grey, L. (1968). *A new approach to discipline: Logical consequences.* New York: Hawthorne.

Dreikurs, R., Grundwald, B., & Pepper, F. (1982). *Maintaining sanity in the classroom: Classroom management techniques* (2nd ed.). New York: Harper & Row.

Evertson, C. (1982). Differences in instructional activities in higher- and lower-achieving junior high English and math classes. *Elementary School Journal, 82,* 329–350.

Evertson, C. (1987). Managing classrooms: A framework for teachers. In D. Berliner & B. Rosenshine (Eds.), *Talks to teachers* (pp. 54–75). New York: Random House.

Farrar, M. (1986). Teacher questions: The complexity of the cognitively simple. *Instructional Science, 15,* 89–107.

French, J. R. P., & Raven, B. (1960). The bases of social power. In D. Cartwright & A. Zander (Eds.), *Group dynamics: Research and theory* (2nd ed., pp. 607–623). Evanston, IL: Row-Peterson.

Furlong, M., & Smith, D. (Eds.). (1994). *Anger, hostility, and aggression: Assessment, prevention, and intervention strategies for youth.* Brandon, VT: Clinical Psychology Publishing.

Gall, M. (1984). Synthesis of research on teachers' questioning. *Educational Leadership, 42*(3), 40–47.

Ginott, H. G. (1972). *Teacher and child: A book for parents and teachers.* New York: Macmillan.

Good, T. L., & Brophy, J. E. (2008). *Looking in classrooms* (10th ed.). Boston: Pearson.

Good, T. L., & Weinstein, R. (1986). Teacher expectations: A framework for exploring classrooms. In K. K. Zumwalt (Ed.), *Improving teaching* (The 1986 ASCD Yearbook, pp. 63–86). Alexandria, VA: Association for Supervision and Curriculum Development.

Gordon, T. (1989). *Teaching children self-discipline at home and in school.* New York: Random House.

Grabe, M. (1985). Attributions in a mastery instructional system: Is an emphasis on effort harmful? *Contemporary Educational Psychology, 10,* 113–126.

Groisser, P. (1964). *How to use the fine art of questioning.* Valley Stream, NY: Teachers Practical Press.

Jones, F. (1992). *Positive classroom discipline.* New York: McGraw-Hill.

Jones, V., & Jones, L. (2001). *Comprehensive classroom management: Creating communities of support and solving problems* (6th ed.). Boston: Allyn & Bacon.

Kohlberg, L. (1969). *Stages in the development of moral thought and action.* New York: Holt, Rinehart & Winston.

Kohn, A. (2006a). *Beyond discipline: From compliance to community, 10th anniversary edition.* Alexandria, VA: Association for Supervision and Curriculum Development.

Kohn, A. (2006b). *The homework myth: Why our kids get too much of a bad thing.* Cambridge, MA: Da Capo Press.

Kounin, J. S. (1970). *Discipline and group management in classrooms.* New York: Holt, Rinehart & Winston.

Levin, J., & Nolan, J. F. (2007). *Principles of classroom management: A professional decision-making model* (5th ed.). Boston: Allyn & Bacon.

Levin, J., & Shanken-Kaye, J. (2002). *From disrupter to achiever: Creating successful learning environments for the self-control classroom.* Dubuque, IA: Kendall/Hunt.

Maslow, A. (1968). *Toward a psychology of being.* New York: Van Nostrand.

Nelson, J. (1987). *Positive discipline*. New York: Ballantine.

Novak, J. D. (1998). *Learning, creating, and using knowledge: Concept maps as facilitative tools in schools and corporations*. Mahwah, NJ: Erlbaum.

Novak, J. D., & Gowin, D. B. (1984). *Learning how to learn*. New York: Cambridge University Press.

Piaget, J. (1965). *The moral judgment of the child*. New York: Free Press.

Rowe, M. B. (1986). Wait time: Slowing down may be a way of speeding up! *Journal of Teacher Education, 37*(1), 43–50.

Saphier, J., & Gower, R. (1982). *The skillful teacher*. Carlisle, MA: Research for Better Teaching.

Sullivan, K., Cleary, M., & Sullivan, G. (2004). *Bullying in secondary schools: What it looks like and how to manage it*. London: Chapman.

Tanner, L. N. (1978). *Classroom discipline for effective teaching and learning*. New York: Holt, Rinehart & Winston.

Tobin, K. (1990). *Metaphors and images in teaching* (What Research Says to the Science and Mathematics Teacher, No. 5). Perth, Western Australia: Curtin University of Technology, The Key Centre for School Science and Mathematics.

Vygotsky, L. (1962). *Thought and language*. Cambridge, MA: MIT Press.

Glossary and Index of Technical Terms

Note: A bold font, such as **P** for Preface, **C** for Conclusion, or the numeral for a particular chapter, follows each definition to indicate where in the book the concept is defined or its meaning elaborated.

Bullying A form of physical, psychological, or social violence in which a group or individual targets for abuse the person or property of another group or individual perceived as vulnerable. **22**

Class Clown A student, usually male, who, through his antics, seeks to dominate class interactions in order to gain his classmates' attention. **15**

Classroom Management Establishing and maintaining social order so that instruction and learning can occur. **P, C**

Classroom Manager A teacher who concentrates not on treating misbehavior but on continuing the lesson so as to engage as many students as possible in learning activities. **7, 8, 15, C**

Cycle of Discouragement The cycle in which a student with a history of academic failure misbehaves in order to feel significant, but the consequence of the misbehavior results in a reaffirmed sense of failure and the need to misbehave further. **20**

Dead Time   The time during a lesson when the students are not engaged in a learning activity. **4, 7, 11, C**

Disciplinarian   A teacher who concentrates on treating misbehavior rather than on continuing the lesson. **7, 15**

Discipline Problem   A problem caused by behavior the teacher regards as competing with, disrupting, or threatening to disrupt the lesson. **P**

Do-Now   A daily routine consisting of an activity each student is expected to work on independently for the first few minutes upon entering the classroom so as to get, without the teacher's supervision and even before the bell rings, every student ready to work. **1, 2, 6, 7, 9, 10, 19**

Good Student   A student who understands and accepts classroom rules as reasonable, whose infractions are occasional at most and are the result of forgetfulness or lapses in self-control rather than defiance. **14**

Lesson Execution Problem   A problem caused by the teacher's error in planning, preparing, or executing the lesson. **P**

Logical Consequence   A reasonable outcome the teacher imposes that is directly related to the misbehavior. **9**

Mastery Learning   An instructional approach in which students are each given the time and support to master a set of concepts or skills at their current academic level before progressing to the next level. **20**

Misbehavior   Behavior the teacher regards as competing with, disrupting, or threatening to disrupt the lesson. **P, 29, C**

Novice Teacher   A teacher with fewer than 3 years of teaching experience. **P, 1, 10, 16, 24, 25, C**

Overlapping   A teacher's attending to two or more situations or tasks simultaneously. **24, C**

Physically Safe Learning Environment   An environment in which the teacher models and the students practice techniques to protect themselves, each other, and the environment from physical harm. **11**

Planned Ignoring   A strategy in which the teacher notices a behavior but intentionally and completely ignores it. **27**

Planning for the Content   Refers to the teacher's defining the lesson objective and then devising a set of activities in which the students can construct the knowledge in that objective and then, along with the teacher, assess whether they have constructed the knowledge as intended. **2**

Planning for the Execution   Refers to the teacher's determining how (and sometimes when) during a lesson to take attendance, divide the students into groups, distribute and collect materials, give directions, and so forth. **2**

Practical Knowledge   Experiential knowledge, the knowledge that is bound up in the perception of details, the knowledge that is concrete and directly applicable to practice. **P**

Proactive Management Strategy   A strategy to prevent a threat to or actual breach of order. **18, C**

Proximity Interference   The teacher's moving toward the source of disruption without interrupting the lesson. **17**

Reactive Management Strategy   A strategy designed to stop or punish a threat to or actual breach of order. **18, C**

Recitation   A series of teacher questions, each followed by a student's answer, often resulting in a monotonous stream of trivial questions, which, at any one time, calls for the participation of only one student. **3, 8, 12, 15, 18, 27**

Revenge-Seeking Students   Students who, feeling that they have no control over their environment and that others disregard them and treat them unfairly, are likely to erupt with anger and abuse in response to a teacher's demand or reprimand. **25**

Routine   A set of procedures (with implicit behavioral expectations) to execute a regular classroom activity. **2, 9, 10, 11, C**

Signal Interference   A nonverbal intervention, such as eye contact or other gesture, that discreetly communicates to the student that the behavior is inappropriate. **17**

Socially and Psychologically Safe Learning Environment An environment in which students interact respectfully and supportively, and each feels valued and capable of both learning and contributing to the learning of others. **11, 22**

Story   A narrative that imbues a set of events with meaning. **P**

Theoretical Knowledge   The knowledge expressed in generalizations, such as the knowledge teacher candidates construct during their teacher preparation coursework. **P**

Time-Out   A break without consequences in response to a student's mounting stress and providing an opportunity for the student to gain composure before returning to class. **17, 26**

Touch Interference   Light, nonaggressive physical contact with an object near the student, such as a series of taps on the student's book or desk. **17**

Wait Time 1   The length of the pause between a teacher's asking a question and calling on a student to answer. **8**

Wait Time 2   The length of the pause between a student's answer and the teacher's response to that answer. **8**

Withitness   The ability of teachers to communicate to their students that they know what their students are up to. **24**

Alphabetical Index of Practical Principles

Note: A bold font, such as **P** for Preface, **C** for Conclusion, or the numeral for a particular chapter, follows each practical principle to indicate where in the book the principle is mentioned.

A novice teacher can avert the discipline problems consequential to all but the most egregious planning shortfalls. **5**

A penetrating comment may be necessary to remind students when they are not living up to expectations or their responsibilities. **19, 20, 22**

A private conversation preserves the student's or students' dignity, thereby forestalling a defensive or hostile response. **15, 17, 18, 22, 23, 24, 25, 26, 27**

A teacher can regain students' interest by involving them in an appealing learning activity. **8, 9**

A teacher needs to consider both management and curricular objectives when planning and executing a lesson. **7, 18, C**

A teacher needs to make sure that students understand the problem from the teacher's perspective and that he or she understands it from theirs. **17, 18, 27**

A teacher should be strict about students' behavior but permissive about their feelings. **13, 17, 24, 26**

A "working with" rather than a "doing to" approach promotes student maturity. **4, 7, 14, 16, 17, 19, 21, 22, 23, 25, 27, 28**

Activities in which students can work together, choose their task, be creative, use novel materials, imagine a novel situation, or relate a concept to everyday life appeal to students. **2, 11**

Address the situation, not the shortcomings of the student(s). **1, 7, 8, 14, 18, 22, 25**

An administrative intervention should be reserved for an emergency. **7, 22, 29**

An appealing lesson is necessary but not sufficient to preclude most discipline problems. **P, C**

Check for understanding frequently and be ready to explain the basics. **4**

Cleaning up should never be left for the very end of a class. **9, 11**

Communicating high expectations is likely to improve student behavior as well as achievement. **15, 17, 18, 26**

Dead time generates disorder. **4, 7, C**

Difficult tasks perceived as meaningless generate frustration and consequently disorder. **4**

Do not make the success of your lesson dependent on all your students having done their homework. **10**

Don't be afraid to admit your mistakes. **12, 16, 19, 22**

Enhancing chronically disruptive students' feelings of significance might, over time, improve their behavior. **20**

Everyone need not complete every learning task, just its essential parts. **5**

Everyone needs to be quiet for the Silence Signal to work. **6**

Execute your decisions with the conviction of a baseball umpire. **17, 18**

For every minute you divert your students from the course of your lesson, you will lose several times that amount trying to reengage them. **12, 17**

Give a class clown attention but for only appropriate behavior. **15**

Good discipline is achieved only through repeated kindnesses. **14, 19, 26**

Hands-on is not enough; the task also has to be brains-on. **4, 9**

Have handy, for both you and your students, extra supplies and equipment. **12**

Having students work in pairs (with teacher support) is particularly useful for low achievers, who can then teach each other without the fear of making a mistake publicly. **1**

Honest communication is fundamental to your relationships with your students. **12, 19**

Humor defuses tension and promotes a positive relationship with students but only when directed at the teacher or a situation, never at a student. **3**

If students have made a commitment to a rule, especially one they had a share in creating, they are likely to correct their misbehavior with simply a reminder of the rule. **15, 17, 26, 27**

If students must hold a piece of equipment so you can instruct them in its use, then distribute just that piece of equipment. **9**

If used consistently, a routine minimizes the time and energy needed to direct a regular classroom event. **2, 6, 9, 10, 11, C**

Ignore behaviors that hardly interfere with teaching or learning. **14, 25, 27**

Instead of criticizing the actions of their students, teachers can safely express their anger by referring to their own feelings. **22, 23, 25, 27**

Issuing an order promotes defiance, not cooperation. **14, 25**

Make the connection between instructional segments explicit to your students. **1**

Materials should be distributed no sooner than immediately before each student or group is to use them, and they should be collected no later than immediately after each student or group is finished with them. **9**

Never impose group punishment. **4, 8, 22**

Never leave your class unattended. **24**

No matter what 3- to 5-minute activity or activities you regularly use for your do-now, your students should be able to find the written directions themselves, in the same place every day, as they enter your classroom. **6**

Nonverbal signals are better than verbal signals because they do not provoke defensive arguments or hostile confrontations. **7, 8, 9, 11, 17, 27** Nonverbal signals also do not interrupt the flow of the lesson, and they invite the students to control their own behavior. **7, 17, 27**

Novice teachers have difficulty claiming their power as the authority. **7, 18, 19, 24**

Offering a choice fosters autonomy rather than dependency and lessens defiance. **17, 18, 20, 21, 25, 26**

Only when you recognize your own contribution to a problem do you have any power to solve it. **2, 4, 8, 12, 16, 19, 25, 28**

Preparation and organization are crucial to the execution of an activity-based lesson. **1, C**

Proactive management strategies are better than reactive management strategies. **18, 23, 24, C**

Punctuating a lecture with thought-provoking questions (typically "why," "how," or "what if" questions) can stimulate interest. **3, 12**

Punishment does not deter misbehavior; it fosters resentment, not cooperation. **4, 7, 8, 14, 17, 18, 25, 26, 27**

Quickening the pace of a lesson is a useful technique but only when the potential for boredom is high, such as during a lecture or recitation, and the students are efficient learners who care about their grades. **8**

Rather than impose control, a teacher should foster students' self-control. **7, 8, 9, 14, 16, 27**

Resist the impulse to attribute minor infractions to defiance. **14**

Resist the tendency to take your students' misbehaviors personally. **7, 19, 26**

Strategies for the short term may be necessary, but they are rarely sufficient. **C**

Students appreciate a novel activity as long as its meaning has been made explicit. **1**

Students appreciate learning about a concept they can relate to everyday life. **3**

Students are likely to abide by a rule they had a share in creating. **9**

Students are likely to abide by rules if they have had the opportunity to understand and agree to them. **7, 11**

Students are most receptive to feedback immediately after they complete a task. **20**

Students can listen for only a short period of time. Then they need an opportunity to build their own understanding of the material. **8**

Students need a set of written directions. **4, 9**

Students need opportunities to learn and practice a routine. **9, 11**

Students need specific and immediate feedback to recognize their behavior. **19, 28**

Students need to produce some evidence of cognitive work during an activity. **9**

Students need to understand the rationale behind a rule, routine, or expectation, that each is not simply an arbitrary attempt to control their behavior. **9, 11, 14, 15, 17, 23, 25**

Teach (by example); don't preach. **25**

Teachers are more likely to be successful with students who see the teacher as on their side. **14, 18, 22, 25, 26, 28**

Teachers are responsible for providing a standard of care commensurate with their students' maturity and the hazards of the activity. **11**

Teachers can strengthen a signal with multiple cues. **6, 17, 24**

Teachers cannot control their students' behaviors, although they can influence and react to them. **5, 7, 8, 25, 27** Teachers can, however, control their own behavior. **5, 7, 8, 25**

Teachers need a systematic management plan ranging from subtle to progressively more direct and intrusive interventions. **14, 17, 18, 20, 27**

Teachers need to be the model of a rational, temperate, consistent, and positive adult, the only such model some of their students may ever see. **12, 19, 22, 23**

Teachers need to recognize and accept their limitations. **13, 21**

The development of a trusting relationship with a caring adult is the most effective strategy for treating a student with a chronic school problem. **20, 25, 27**

The do-now must be an activity that requires students to sit down and take out their notebook, perhaps their textbook, and a pencil or pen. **1, 6, 7**

The promise of redemption is a strong motivator. **17, 20, 28**

The teacher needs to have a definite plan for every activity. **5**

There's always a tomorrow. . . . Leave the problem at school. **C**

To safeguard relationships with their students, teachers need to be careful, especially when angry, to express how they feel without deprecating their students. **16, 22**

Unstructured time generates boredom, restlessness, and disruption. **2, 9, 17, 24**

Using threats (or bribes) to control student behavior undermines any potential for a mutually respectful relationship. **4, 17, 18, 25, 27**

Welcome the expression of your students' feelings as feedback to improve your teaching. **3, 19**

When class periods are longer, timing errors compound. **5**

Whenever you have some students monopolizing the class's time, you need to decentralize instruction. **4, 15, 18, 27**

Your first priority is to protect the other students and yourself. Your second priority is to protect the students who are fighting. Your third priority is to protect property. **24**

Topical Index of Practical Principles

Note: The set of practical principles has been divided into five categories: Practical principles about (1) Building Relationships With Students, (2) Discipline, (3) Lesson Execution, (4) Lesson Planning, and (5) Teachers. A bold font, such as **P** for Preface, **C** for Conclusion, or the numeral for a particular chapter, follows each practical principle to indicate where in the book the principle is mentioned. Some principles have been assigned to more than one category.

BUILDING RELATIONSHIPS WITH STUDENTS

A teacher should be strict about students' behavior but permissive about their feelings. **13, 17, 24, 26**

A "working with" rather than a "doing to" approach promotes student maturity. **4, 7, 14, 16, 17, 19, 21, 22, 23, 25, 27, 28**

Don't be afraid to admit your mistakes. **12, 16, 19, 22**

Enhancing chronically disruptive students' feelings of significance might, over time, improve their behavior. **20**

Honest communication is fundamental to your relationships with your students. **12, 19**

Humor defuses tension and promotes a positive relationship with students but only when directed at the teacher or a situation, never at a student. **3**

Instead of criticizing the actions of their students, teachers can safely express their anger by referring to their own feelings. **22, 23, 25, 27**

Offering a choice fosters autonomy rather than dependency and lessens defiance. **17, 18, 20, 21, 25, 26**

Students are most receptive to feedback immediately after they complete a task. **20**

Teachers are more likely to be successful with students who see the teacher as on their side. **14, 18, 22, 25, 26, 28**

The development of a trusting relationship with a caring adult is the most effective strategy for treating a student with a chronic school problem. **20, 25, 27**

To safeguard relationships with their students, teachers need to be careful, especially when angry, to express how they feel without deprecating their students. **16, 22**

Welcome the expression of your students' feelings as feedback to improve your teaching. **3, 19**

DISCIPLINE

A penetrating comment may be necessary to remind students when they are not living up to expectations or their responsibilities. **19, 20, 22**

A private conversation preserves the student's or students' dignity, thereby forestalling a defensive or hostile response. **15, 17, 18, 22, 23, 24, 25, 26, 27**

A teacher needs to make sure that students understand the problem from the teacher's perspective and that he or she understands it from theirs. **17, 18, 27**

Address the situation, not the shortcomings of the student(s). **1, 7, 8, 14, 18, 22, 25**

An administrative intervention should be reserved for an emergency. **7, 22, 29**

An appealing lesson is necessary but not sufficient to preclude most discipline problems. **P, C**

Communicating high expectations is likely to improve student behavior as well as achievement. **15, 17, 18, 26**

Give a class clown attention but for only appropriate behavior. **15**

Good discipline is achieved only through repeated kindnesses. **14, 19, 26**

If students have made a commitment to a rule, especially one they had a share in creating, they are likely to correct their misbehavior with simply a reminder of the rule. **15, 17, 26, 27**

Ignore behaviors that hardly interfere with teaching or learning. **14, 25, 27**

Issuing an order promotes defiance, not cooperation. **14, 25**

Never impose group punishment. **4, 8, 22**

Nonverbal signals are better than verbal signals because they do not provoke defensive arguments or hostile confrontations. **7, 8, 9, 11, 17, 27** Nonverbal signals also do not interrupt the flow of the lesson, and they invite the students to control their own behavior. **7, 17, 27**

Offering a choice fosters autonomy rather than dependency and lessens defiance. **17, 18, 20, 21, 25, 26**

Proactive management strategies are better than reactive management strategies. **18, 23, 24, C**

Punishment does not deter misbehavior; it fosters resentment, not cooperation. **4, 7, 8, 14, 17, 18, 25, 26, 27**

Rather than impose control, a teacher should foster students' self-control. **7, 8, 9, 14, 16, 27**

Resist the impulse to attribute minor infractions to defiance. **14**

Resist the tendency to take your students' misbehaviors personally. **7, 19, 26**

Strategies for the short term may be necessary, but they are rarely sufficient. **C**

Students are likely to abide by a rule they had a share in creating. **9**

Students are likely to abide by rules if they have had the opportunity to understand and agree to them. **7, 11**

Students need specific and immediate feedback to recognize their behavior. **19, 28**

Students need to understand the rationale behind a rule, routine, or expectation, that each is not simply an arbitrary attempt to control their behavior. **9, 11, 14, 15, 17, 23, 25**

Teach (by example); don't preach. **25**

Teachers need a systematic management plan ranging from subtle to progressively more direct and intrusive interventions. **14, 17, 18, 20, 27**

The promise of redemption is a strong motivator. **17, 20, 28**

Using threats (or bribes) to control student behavior undermines any potential for a mutually respectful relationship. **4, 17, 18, 25, 27**

Your first priority is to protect the other students and yourself. Your second priority is to protect the students who are fighting. Your third priority is to protect property. **24**

Lesson Execution

A teacher can regain students' interest by involving them in an appealing learning activity. **8, 9**

A teacher needs to consider both management and curricular objectives when planning and executing a lesson. **7, 18, C**

Check for understanding frequently and be ready to explain the basics. **4**

Cleaning up should never be left for the very end of a class. **9, 11**

Dead time generates disorder. **4, 7, C**

Difficult tasks perceived as meaningless generate frustration and consequently disorder. **4**

Everyone need not complete every learning task, just its essential parts. **5**

Everyone needs to be quiet for the Silence Signal to work. **6**

Execute your decisions with the conviction of a baseball umpire. **17, 18**

For every minute you divert your students from the course of your lesson, you will lose several times that amount trying to reengage them. **12, 17**

Have handy, for both you and your students, extra supplies and equipment. **12**

Having students work in pairs (with teacher support) is particularly useful for low achievers, who can then teach each other without the fear of making a mistake publicly. **1**

If students must hold a piece of equipment so you can instruct them in its use, then distribute just that piece of equipment. **9**

If used consistently, a routine minimizes the time and energy needed to direct a regular classroom event. **2, 6, 9, 10, 11, C**

Make the connection between instructional segments explicit to your students. **1**

Materials should be distributed no sooner than immediately before each student or group is to use them, and they should be collected no later than immediately after each student or group is finished with them. **9**

Never leave your class unattended. **24**

No matter what 3- to 5-minute activity or activities you regularly use for your do-now, your students should be able to find the written directions themselves, in the same place every day, as they enter your classroom. **6**

Preparation and organization are crucial to the execution of an activity-based lesson. **1, C**

Punctuating a lecture with thought-provoking questions (typically "why," "how," or "what if" questions) can stimulate interest. **3, 12**

Quickening the pace of a lesson is a useful technique but only when the potential for boredom is high, such as during a lecture or recitation, and the students are efficient learners who care about their grades. **8**

Students appreciate a novel activity as long as its meaning has been made explicit. **1**

Students need a set of written directions. **4, 9**

Students need opportunities to learn and practice a routine. **9, 11**

Whenever you have some students monopolizing the class's time, you need to decentralize instruction. **4, 15, 18, 27**

LESSON PLANNING

A novice teacher can avert the discipline problems consequential to all but the most egregious planning shortfalls. **5**

A teacher needs to consider both management and curricular objectives when planning and executing a lesson. **7, 18, C**

Activities in which students can work together, choose their task, be creative, use novel materials, imagine a novel situation, or relate a concept to everyday life appeal to students. **2, 11**

An appealing lesson is necessary but not sufficient to preclude most discipline problems. **P, C**

Do not make the success of your lesson dependent on all your students having done their homework. **10**

Hands-on is not enough; the task also has to be brains-on. **4, 9**

Punctuating a lecture with thought-provoking questions (typically "why," "how," or "what if" questions) can stimulate interest. **3, 12**

Students appreciate a novel activity as long as its meaning has been made explicit. **1**

Students appreciate learning about a concept they can relate to everyday life. **3**

Students can listen for only a short period of time. Then they need an opportunity to build their own understanding of the material. **8**

Students need to produce some evidence of cognitive work during an activity. **9**

The do-now must be an activity that requires students to sit down and take out their notebook, perhaps their textbook, and a pencil or pen **1, 6, 7**

The teacher needs to have a definite plan for every activity. **5**

Unstructured time generates boredom, restlessness, and disruption. **2, 9, 17, 24**

When class periods are longer, timing errors compound. **5**

Whenever you have some students monopolizing the class's time, you need to decentralize instruction. **4, 15, 18, 27**

TEACHERS

A novice teacher can avert the discipline problems consequential to all but the most egregious planning short-falls. **5**

Novice teachers have difficulty claiming their power as the authority. **7, 18, 19, 24**

Only when you recognize your own contribution to a problem do you have any power to solve it. **2, 4, 8, 12, 16, 19, 25, 28**

Teachers cannot control their students' behaviors, although they can influence and react to them. **5, 7, 8, 25, 27** Teachers can, however, control their own behavior. **5, 7, 8, 25**

Teachers need to be the model of a rational, temperate, consistent, and positive adult, the only such model some of their students may ever see. **12, 19, 22, 23**

Teachers need to recognize and accept their limitations. **13, 21**

There's always a tomorrow. . . . Leave the problem at school. **C**

Index of Supplementary Concepts

Note: Every chapter features at least one supplementary note in which a concept related to one or more of the stories is identified with references. The bold numeral following each concept label is the number of the chapter in which that concept is identified.

General Index

Active lessons, 46, 54
   See also Activity-based lessons
Activity-based lessons, xviii,
   2, 7, 8, 177
   See also Active lessons
Administrative interventions. *See*
   Interventions, administrative
Adolescent conflict resolution,
   145 (note)
Anger, student, 104, 142, 151 (note)
Anger, teacher
   compassion instead of, 85, 120
   expressing safely, xviii, 97, 133,
      139, 140 (note), 149, 162–163
   response to emotional
      involvement, 129–130
   response to misbehavior, 113,
      162–163, 167
   waiting to express, 121, 139

Block scheduling, 30, 59
Boredom. *See* Student boredom
Brophy, J. E., 70 (note)
Bullough, R. V., Jr., xviii, 33 (note),
   144 (note)
Bullying, 131, 133, 135–136
   bullying triangle, 136 (note)

Canter, L., 88 (note)
Canter, M., 88 (note)
Class clown, xx, 89–93, 94 (note)
Classroom management, xii, xv
   14, 29, 55, 174
   examples of proactive, 44,
      110–111, 112, 113, 114 (note),
      138, 142, 166

   proactive as opposed to reactive,
      110–111, 138, 175
   reactive strategies, 110, 113, 114
      (note), 138, 142, 175
Classroom manager
   as opposed to disciplinarian, 38,
      40, 50, 56, 91, 174–178
   strategies of, 43, 44, 50, 174–178
   See also Disciplinarian
Cleary, M., 136 (note)
Cognitive burden, 22–23
Community. *See* Learning
   community
Concept mapping, 12, 13 (note)
Cooperation
   fostering, 86–87, 97, 147, 151
   as opposed to resentment, 26, 42,
      58, 104, 113
Crimes, 172, 173 (note)
   See also Misbehavior, as opposed
      to crimes; Violence
Cycle of discouragement, 126
   (note)

Dead time, 21–22, 45, 74, 177
Detention, 39, 48, 136, 152, 164,
   173, 178
Dictator, 44, 97, 177
   See also Roles, teacher
Disciplinarian, 38, 40, 44, 56, 91
   See also Classroom manager, as
      opposed to disciplinarian;
      Misbehavior
Discipline, 51, 175
   challenges to, 10, 148
   and kindness, 85, 121, 158

203

CORWIN

A SAGE Company

The Corwin logo—a raven striding across an open book—represents the union of courage and learning. Corwin is committed to improving education for all learners by publishing books and other professional development resources for those serving the field of PreK–12 education. By providing practical, hands-on materials, Corwin continues to carry out the promise of its motto: **"Helping Educators Do Their Work Better."**